MW01181691

ASPATORE
Executive Business Intelligence

About Aspatore
Executive Business Intelligence
www.Aspatore.com

Aspatore publishes only the biggest names in the business world, including C-Level leaders (CEO, CTO, CFO, COO, CMO, Partner) from over half the world's 500 largest companies and other leading executives. Aspatore publishes a highly innovative line of business intelligence brands including Inside the Minds, Bigwig Briefs, Focusbook, ExecRecs, Brainstormers, What Ifs, IdeaJournal, CareerJournal, Business Travel Bible and Aspatore Business Reviews, in addition to other best selling business books, journals and briefs. By focusing on publishing only the biggest name executives, Aspatore provides readers with proven business intelligence from industry insiders, rather than relying on the knowledge of unknown authors and analysts. Aspatore focuses on publishing traditional print books with individuals, while our portfolio companies, Corporate Publishing Group (B2B publisher) and ExecEnablers (retail business intelligence stores) focus on developing areas within the business and book publishing worlds. Aspatore is committed to providing our readers, authors, bookstores, distributors and customers with the highest quality books, journals, briefs and publishing execution available anywhere in the world.

The *Bigwig Briefs* Series
Condensed Business Intelligence From Industry Insiders
www.BigwigBriefs.com

Bigwig Briefs features condensed business intelligence from industry insiders and are the best way for business professionals to stay on top of the most pressing issues. *Bigwig Briefs* features knowledge excerpts from the best selling business books published by Aspatore books, other leading business book publishers, and essays written by leading executives for inclusion in a particular brief. *Bigwig Briefs* is revolutionizing the business book market by providing the highest quality content in the most condensed format possible for business book readers worldwide.

B I G W I G   B R I E F S

BIGWIG BRIEFS:
SMALL BUSINESS
MARKETING ADVISOR

*Big Business Marketing Secrets That Can and Should Be
Used By Small Businesses*

ASPATORE
Executive Business Intelligence

Published by Aspatore Books, Inc.

For information on bulk orders, sponsorship opportunities or any other questions please email store@aspatore.com. For corrections, company/title updates, comments or any other inquiries please email info@aspatore.com.

First Printing, 2002
10 9 8 7 6 5 4 3 2 1

ISBN 1-58762-203-3

Edited By Ginger Conlon

Cover design by Rachel Kashon, Kara Yates

BIGWIG BRIEFS

BIGWIG BRIEFS:
SMALL BUSINESS
MARKETING ADVISOR

*Big Business Marketing Secrets That Can and Should Be
Used By Small Businesses*

ASPATORE
Executive Business Intelligence

Published by Aspatore Books, Inc.
For information on bulk orders, sponsorship opportunities or any other questions please email store@aspatore.com. For corrections, company/title updates, comments or any other inquiries please email info@aspatore.com.

First Printing, 2002
10 9 8 7 6 5 4 3 2 1

ISBN 1-58762-203-3

Edited By Ginger Conlon

Cover design by Rachel Kashon, Kara Yates

BIGWIG BRIEFS:
THE SMALL BUSINESS MARKETING ADVISOR

CONTENTS

BIGWIG BRIEFS:
SMALL BUSINESS
MARKETING ADVISOR

Stephen C. Jones, The Coca-Cola Company, Chief Marketing Officer

Enjoyable Aspects of Marketing

Think of marketing as a series of processes. You begin by assembling qualitative and quantitative data. Second, you convert that data into useful insight. Third, you use those insights as a foundation to build a coherent marketing strategy. You create your plans and then executive that strategy in the marketplace. I've always enjoyed the process of creating new ideas for consumers to engage in the brand life. It's the most dynamic process.

The second part of marketing that is fun is the leadership – pulling together people who really understand what we are all trying to achieve to create a collaborative network that can produce results. I hope to be recognized for bringing together the right people, figuring out the idea that we are going to pursue, and helping them make it happen. To me, that's where the fun comes from – allowing other people to be successful.

Creating Ties With Consumers and Then Connecting With Them

The process of gaining insight has to be very local. It would be a mistake to try to centralize the process of connecting with consumers. You have to have the best quality people who are well trained out in the marketplace, talking to people. This isn't just traditional qualitative and quantitative research methodology that I am talking about; I am talking about marketers who are on the street, in people's homes, and living in the community, so that they really understand the rhythms and nuances of daily life. We have a community of marketers around the world, each with a deep understanding of his or her own market, and each of whom is responsible for getting that insight. We can provide them with thought models and techniques and protocol on how to go get insight, but we leave it to them to detect trends and then translate them into opportunities around which we build our initiatives. I don't do that personally; I rely on marketers around the world to do that.

Connecting with people happens in a number of ways. The connection starts by making sure that the product you have is one people want and need and that it is a great product. Coca-Cola is a great-tasting, refreshing, thirst-quenching beverage that can't be copied. It has a unique flavor. It's absolutely dependable. You can trust in the product. That's essential in order to make the first connection.

We also connect through the positioning of the brand and the core values. Coke is about much more than quenching one's thirst; it's about a magical refreshment of one's body, mind, and spirit. There are certain things that the brand stands for. It is very alive. We need to connect with people through activities that are very alive. We choose to associate with sports, entertainment, and music because those are things that people are passionate about, and those are also things that can connect with the core values of the brand.

We connect with people on a day-to-day basis by ensuring that we are available to them as they go through their daily lives. We are determined to be everywhere people are going to be. The connections are made through advertising communications, and promotions. We are changing the way we promote – moving away from a concentration on the big wins and sweepstakes and toward a greater focus on becoming more relevant to consumers on a day-to-day basis. We want to make a daily connection with Coke's consumers – in a way that is relevant in their lives.

What Constitutes a Successful Marketing Campaign

Success is largely determined by the objectives you set for yourself at the beginning. However, while achieving the goal is very important, the way in which you get there – the creativity, innovativeness, leadership, substance, and value created – promises longer-term benefits than those derived from simply achieving those short-term goals. If you can achieve your basic, fundamental objectives and goals and do it in a way that creates long-term relationships with people, where people are prepared to make a commitment back to a brand, then that is really true success.

There is another one. It isn't about the consumer; it is about the people who work on the brands. When people who put the stuff together, whether they are financial managers, salesmen, or brand managers, when they feel they have done something worthwhile and improved the state of somebody's life or the quality of the company, then that is another measure of success.

Skills Needed on the Marketing Team

We want the same thing everybody else does; we just want more, better, and faster. First of all, I think every company has a different culture and attracts a certain type of person. At Coke, culture is fairly strong. We want people to be a part of the culture.

Second, we want a lot of diversity – a lot of people with a lot of different ideas who can approach things from different directions. There is never just one solution. Diversity of thinking is critical in the type of people we are looking for.

In addition to people who will become part of our culture and add to the diversity of that culture, we want skills. We want really bright people who are terribly ambitious about making success happen – not just for themselves, but also for the team and company around them. They need to be curious and inventive and driven in an incredibly fast-paced, complex world.

Finally, we want people who want to make things happen fast, who aren't afraid to execute, who take action on good ideas. Those are the people we need to build a team around the world.

Golden Rules of Marketing

Consumers are at the center of everything we do. Everything we own in the brand is essential to maintain our commitment to the quality, integrity, and values of the brand. In the end, people are making all their choices based on what that brand stands for. Make sure you are continuously investing in the core essence of what the brand stands for.

Trust, respect, commitment, and collaboration of the people who are designing the market – this must always be maintained at the highest level to get anything decent or creative executed.

T. Michael Glenn, FedEx Corporation, Executive Vice President, Market Development & Corporate Communications

---

Most Important Elements of Marketing

To be successful in marketing, you have to develop your company's value proposition in a way that meets or exceeds the customer's requirements and expectations. You also must have a value delivery system that ensures your message breaks through. If you are successful, your company is going to meet the market's requirements. Marketing is not rocket science. It's more common sense than anything else, but it's amazing how many people don't have the ability to sit down and understand what customers are really looking for.

For example, look back at the dot-bombs. If those companies had had a clear understanding of what the consumer really wanted and made sure their value proposition was solid, they would have saved themselves a lot of time and money. Customers will always tell you if your product or service is going to work. Just listen to them. The rest is blocking and tackling.

Looking to the Consumer for What They Want

There is a cartoon that our chairman likes to quote. It's a Pogo cartoon, and Pogo's claim-to-fame leadership principle is to find a parade and jump in front of it. That's really what we try to do at FedEx. We try to stay in tune with our customers' needs and deliver the solution before anyone else can. In the case of the transition of our brand from Federal Express to FedEx, customers made the switch before we did. If they wanted to refer to us as FedEx, why try to stop them? This demonstrates that when you take the time to listen to your customers, they will tell you what they want. You have to be smart enough to listen, however, and then have the courage to act upon it.

Clear and Simple Marketing Messages

Research supports the fact that a customer can't remember much about a brand, especially if you're relying solely on advertising to communicate the key attributes of your brand. I can reel off several key attributes that set FedEx apart from our competition, but it is difficult to effectively convey them in a print ad, a 30-second commercial, a direct-marketing campaign, or a Web-based campaign. You have to develop two to three key messages that you want to leave with the customer, regardless of the medium used. And the key to developing those messages is understanding what motivates the customer to buy.

In the case of FedEx, our key message is reliability. Once customers start using us based on our reliability, a relationship is established with the customer. And from that established relationship, there is plenty of opportunity over time to communicate some or all of the key attributes that set us apart from the competition.

The Marketing Role in a Company

Marketing's primary role in any organization is to be the customer's advocate. There are always advocates in a company for cutting costs, operational issues, etc. However, the most important job for a marketing executive is to be the chief customer advocate – someone who is willing to fight for the customer at almost any cost. Doing battle on the customers' behalf may not always be pleasant, but I've found that what's in the best interest of the customer is usually in the best interest of the company.

By clearly understanding the needs of the customer and communicating them within the organization, the marketing executive can keep the value proposition fresh and the brand relevant.

All Employees Are Marketers

It's important to understand that everyone represents the brand and has an opportunity to make a positive or negative impact on the brand. In the case of our company, we may have a situation where we deliver a package late due to bad weather. If the courier walks in with a positive attitude and expresses apologies to the customer, the customer is more likely to accept the situation and appreciate the courier's commitment to delivering the package under adverse circumstances. On the other hand, if that courier comes in with a negative attitude because he is working in bad weather, that will have a negative impact on the customer.

Strategically, the chief executive must set the tone for any organization, especially a service organization. He or she must let it be known that in terms of the service experience nothing less than absolute customer delight can be accepted. This philosophy then filters down through the organization. On the other hand, if a CEO lets it be known that he is willing to sacrifice service to save money, that organization will find a lot of ways to cut corners on service.

Michael Linton, Best Buy, Senior Vice President, Strategic Marketing

Branding

Brands exist because they deliver a benefit that is so unique and distinctive that the consumer seeks them out. Great brands usually are so associated with a consumer benefit that they "own that benefit" singularly. Maintaining that benefit requires constant vigilance and work. There are lots of great brands, and they all own a benefit. For example,

Nike probably owns "best shoe for athletic performance." Disney owns "destination for family entertainment," and ESPN owns "destination for televised sports." A brand is "owned" by the millions of consumers who credit it with its benefit and attributes.

If you forget your benefit, don't constantly improve your benefit, or forget to study the target consumer who is at the cutting edge of that benefit, your brand will get passed by new brands that deliver the benefit better and "steal" your consumers. It takes constant effort to keep from losing your way – never forget that your brand has to deliver a benefit better than anyone else to become and stay great.

So marketing never finishes building a brand because brands can always go to the next level. Once you stop improving, you get passed and beaten. Honesty is required to take a brand to the next level – an honest understanding of what your brand is good at and where it is vulnerable. There are a lot of good brands, but few truly dominant brands – brands with huge top-of-mind awareness and a controlling market share position. Brands grow by knowing their position in the marketplace; analyzing market share, share of wallet, and consumer preference; constantly talking to consumers; watching key performance and attitudinal attributes; and studying competition. These are all measures best used with a huge dose of objectivity. I try to look at a broad range of measures and believe it's key to compare measures and performance against your industry as well as world-class performers in other industries.

I am usually very focused on the target consumers. How do they feel about the brand and the benefit? While we sample the general population, we really drill down with the target. For example, many consumers know about the Internet, but the smaller group that has already purchased from Best Buy has a wealth of learning and information for us. How did they use "clicks and mortar"? What did they buy and use next? What problems did they have? That's how we try to stay ahead of that curve. These learnings help us evolve our marketing, product offerings, media, and operating model accordingly.

Jody Bilney, Verizon, Senior Vice President, Brand Management and Marketing Communications

Situations That Can Kill a Brand

Disasters happen and, if mishandled, can kill a brand. For instance, it will be fascinating to see how the whole Firestone situation with the Ford Explorers goes. Today, odds are about 50/50 as to which brand is less damaged and even survives. Another example is years ago when Audi cars sprang into gear by themselves, lurched forward, and pinned people against their garages. At the time that was happening with Audi, they were makers of an upscale foreign car. They were unique and were gaining penetration. I am not sure that this situation was handled very well, or that their brand recovered and had the same position and potential in the marketplace that they might have had before. Not that their brand is dead, but they needed to be more clear on why that happened, how badly they felt about it, and what they did to fix it, so you could trust the Audi brand as a car you want to be driving. There are things that can happen to a brand that, if not handled well, can cause the brand to lose value and relevance. When consumers lose trust, it is very difficult to regain. There are lots of others on the flip side that handled disaster really well and improved their brand's standing. Finally, another way to kill a brand is to stop investing in it.

The Future of Marketing

There are some fundamentals I think will always be there for marketers. Marketers absolutely have to stay in touch with the marketplace, with customers, as well as their competitors. There is no way to do productive marketing without that. You have to pay attention to where customers' heads, habits, and attitudes are and how they are evolving. You can't be an effective marketer if you don't understand who your current and emerging competitors are. This is all about business results at the end of day. I can't see that part ever changing.

Interwoven in both the competitors and customers is the role of the brand. As the world gets faster-paced, and as technology changes, there will be some confusion. The role of the brand becomes more important because it will be the one thing that people understand. They understand they can trust Verizon, and they will get the latest technology at a good value. Interwoven within the customer and the competition, the role of the brand is always going to be there. It is going to play an increasingly important role as our lives get even busier, and technology is changing and evolving. These are the ways marketing is going to stay the same. It will have that constant definition, as long as companies are trying to sell stuff. That's what marketing is going to be all about.

It will probably change in some ways too, because there will be new tools and technology. The Internet is going to continue to evolve. Companies are going to get better at using the Internet for marketing purposes. Someone will figure out that killer app – the combination of privacy and customization. The Internet might be the key to that. There have to be changes, and there will be.

John Hayes, American Express, Executive Vice President, Advertising & Global Brand Management

Killing an Established Brand

A brand does not have an inalienable right. It takes work, nurturing, and a very clear understanding of the consumer. Product failure, slowness in response to product failure, and not completely understanding what the consumer thinks about your brand can kill it.

Many brands have dealt with product failure; some have survived and some haven't. Why? Those who survived quickly recognized product failure, understood what the customer was thinking, and corrected it. That's how you build a brand and keep it alive.

There are three things that can kill an established brand: (1) complacency, (2) assuming a right to exist in the market, and (3) arrogance. A number of companies have gone through bouts of arrogance, thinking they are unassailable, and basically losing touch with the customer base. They no longer know who their customers are, what they need, whether they are getting the right services, and if they have the right balance between cost savings and customer service. Those variables have to be challenged all the time for the brand to remain healthy.

Developing a Marketing Plan

There are some simple steps that we follow that give discipline to the process. The first step is to determine the goal of the project. What are we trying to do – get a million card members, or get people to use the card more? We start off with a very clear articulation of the business goal. To create an effective marketing program, you have to know what you are driving toward. Sometimes it sounds simpler than it is. Sometimes at the beginning of the project the goal has to be clarified.

The second step is defining the target, which we do in two ways: Demographically, by asking the following questions:

Who are they? Where do they live? And, second, by emotional definition, which is personified by American Express Blue. Groups of people were optimistic about the future and eager to embrace technology in their lives. When those two steps are completed, we know what we are trying to do from a business standpoint and whom we are trying to reach.

The third step in our approach is positioning. What is the product we are working with, and how do we position it to make it appealing to the target audience?

The fourth step involves deciding which channels to use for communication. Channel selection depends upon our audience. If we are talking to tech-savvy people, then tech channels will be more useful than they would be to another group. The target audience helps us select the channels for communication. If they are music-savvy, we may use musical events. If they are small-business people using a PC as their connection to the world, we may find that email is the best way to reach them. So we reflect on the target audience and make our channel selection.

Next, we reflect on our goal. If our goal is to reach out to a new group of people and obtain a large number of new card members in a short period, we know we have to go fairly broad on target audience. We also know that our channels have to reflect that approach. We have to create awareness that we have a product for these people, and then we have to take that awareness down to action. Channels are defined by the goal we have established and the target audience. Once we have nailed down the channel, we move to the presentation of the product to the customer, through the channels. Instead of creating a television commercial, we begin by knowing the channels we want to use and create communication that works within them: live events, Internet, direct mail, television, and outdoor posters. The channels have to be nailed down first.

The last steps are creative strategy and ongoing communications. Frequently companies will do a major launch and will not pay attention to ongoing communications and how they continue to nurture a customer base. Finally, we define and measure success. If I have a clear goal, then metrics help me know how I'm doing against it. From the beginning, the measurement of success helps people focus and relates back to the goal. The last piece is brand health. What impact is this going to have on the brand health, and what are the measures? We go into the marketplace and measure the key-initiatives impact the project has had on the brand's health.

Richard Costello, General Electric, Manager, Corporate Marketing Communications

Building an Established Brand

The first component of building an established brand is a promise that is compelling. It is often simple and generic. Let me give you some examples of enduring brands: Coca-Cola, whose basic promise has been refreshment. This is a promise that is simple, compelling, and has been achieved.

Disney promises family entertainment. Marlboro promises satisfaction and a macho, outdoors stereotype. Although they weren't first to take this approach, they have been the most effective and have been able to establish a pretty unassailable position. It is nice to have a unique promise, such as Apple's promise of friendliness to the customer, which is the niche they have taken. Not many people have competed with them in that area. All of the examples are simple and compelling … it is what distinguishes great brands.

The second component is delivering on that promise. When you pick up a Coca-Cola, you get the refreshment of bubbly, fizzy water with a shot of sugar and caffeine. That has delivered refreshment to people every time they take a hit of it. Marlboros deliver great, satisfying cigarette taste to those who smoke; Apple delivers user-friendliness; Disney delivers family entertainment. Disney's promise is so well-established that they can't release an R-rated movie under the Disney brand because it would undermine their entire image. Disney does this under other labels such as Touchstone and Hollywood Pictures. Disney has done maybe one or two PG-13 movies, ever. They understand their promise must be kept … they cannot afford to surprise or disappoint their audience.

The third component is consistency – consistency in the way you communicate your promise over time and consistency in presentation of packaging, environment, and design. The look, feel, and experience have to consistently reinforce the promise you have made, whether the consumer is in the retail environment or sitting in front of a computer screen. The more consistent you are over a period of time, the more effective and cost efficient you are.

An example in the appliance business is Maytag, a competitor of GE's. Maytag has used the symbol of the lonely repairman for 30-plus years. Their advertising has rarely won any awards, but is has been effective in establishing Maytag as a reliable brand that doesn't need repairing. They figured out that reliability of appliance is very important to consumers. The symbol of the lonely repairman communicates reliability to their customers. If you ask people what is the most reliable dishwasher, most people will say a Maytag, and that's a great example of effective branding. They have made a promise, stuck with it for 30 years, and positioned themselves very effectively. We know this because we compete against them.

That concept of consistency also can be demonstrated by Marlboro: It was originally targeted toward women, and it bombed because at that time women were infrequent smokers, and the heavy smokers were men. It shifted to the now familiar cowboy imagery in the early 1950s, and that turned the brand around. I have seen the original cowboy ad in black and white, and it looks virtually identical to today's ads. The only difference is that they are now in color. But it is still Marlboro, and the brand promise has been consistent for 50 years now. Great brands do that.

GE has been making a promise for close to a hundred years that our technology will give you better living. I can show you ads from 1916 that demonstrate how people's lives were improved by using our technology in washing machines, irons, etc. It's a very generic promise of better living, and as early home innovators, we are able to own that simple idea. Over time, our promise has stayed the same. In the 1940s and 1950s our slogan was "Live better electrically," so it was the same idea. Now our slogan is "We bring good things to life." We have played down the electrical aspect now, but the idea remains the same. So over a long period of time, the focus has been on the lifestyle benefits that people get by using our technology rather than the technology itself. That has been a consistent positioning. Those things – consistency of communication, delivery of promise, and a powerful promise that is appealing to a consumer that may or may not be unique – are all important to building a brand.

The Importance of Reinvention for a Brand Name

I think you have to be true to your basic promise and constantly refresh the features. Let's look at Disney. Disney is family entertainment. It started off as cartoons in 1930. When television came around, they added children's entertainment with Disney shows on Sunday. Then they proliferated the brand to an experience by building the first theme park. When that worked, they added a more parks. As they built the parks, they kept refreshing them inside with new and more innovative attractions. Now they have a ship that you can go on for a Disney cruise. They also have hundreds of stores in malls. It is a combination of innovation and broadening the touch points for contact that the consumer may have.

Disney is constantly innovating, but the common theme is that it's for the consumer's family. Their theme parks are high-quality and clean, and they're a good environment for kids. So is every other product ... stores, cruise ships, and movies. They have the old constants like Mickey Mouse and Snow White but constantly introduce new experiences, such as the theme park with real animals down in Florida. They keep coming up with new ideas to keep you there, spending more money and coming back more often, but the basic underlying theme is the same. Great brands do both at the same time: Keep their fundamental promise very much in mind, but think of hundreds of different ways of delivering that promise to you. It is this that keeps the brand fresh and exciting. A great brand is a paradox ... on one hand delivering a singular, consistent promise and on the other a constantly changing series of diverse innovations and variations on the basic theme.

Robyn M. Sachs, RMR & Associates, President and Chief Executive Officer

PR 101: A Necessity, Not a Luxury

What kind of honor is it to be recognized as "Small Business' Best-Kept Secret"? No matter how long you've been in business, customers are less likely to buy from you if they have never heard of your name or product. Name recognition and visibility are the keys to growing your business, and public relations is the way to make your company more visible.

Each big business began as a small company with a plan –
not just a business plan, but an integrated marketing plan,
one that would introduce its products, services, leaders, and
mission into the marketplace using a series of tried-and-true
vehicles. In 1987, when I purchased and became president
of RMR Advertising, a struggling advertising agency, I
knew the only way to climb to the top of our industry was to
do for our own company what we do for our clients: solidify
our internal messaging, create an awareness campaign,
share our firm's message and mission to everyone who
would listen, and do it as frequently as possible. RMR
Advertising is now RMR & Associates, an integrated
advertising, marketing, and public relations agency that
caters to emerging growth companies. When I first
purchased the company we were only a four-person agency.
With a structured plan, a consistent communications effort,
and a lot of enthusiasm, we have grown by 600 percent and
have been recognized as one of the country's fastest-
growing firms.

Even if you don't have a communications powerhouse on
staff, you can still tackle and master the basics of good
public relations, once you have some direction. Public
relations is a necessity, not a luxury, for small businesses.
There are many pieces needed to assemble a well-rounded,
low-cost, high-return public relations program.

The Definition of Small Business

There's no question that small business is a substantial part
of the nation's economy. It may surprise you to know that
90 percent of all U.S. businesses, or roughly 27 million

companies, are small businesses. Small businesses employ 43 million employees, 21 percent of whom are sole proprietors. The official definition of a "small business" fluctuates, but some of the details are clear: The companies have fewer than 100 employees and less than $10 million in revenue. Small businesses also account for $1 trillion in payroll and $5 trillion in annual sales receipts. (Source: The Tower Group, July 2001). It's almost ironic to call the market sector "small" business.

Small businesses compete against not only each other, but also against the giants in the marketplace. That's why PR is so essential; small companies need to make themselves seen and heard in the ever increasing confusion of monster corporations.

The Impact of Public Relations

If a tree falls in the middle of the forest in Oregon, and no one is around to hear it, does it make a noise? It does if an article about that tree is published in *The Register-Guard* and *Oregonian Online* the day it falls. Nothing can disseminate a message, tell a story, rally support, instill confidence, and reinforce loyalty like the third-party credibility that comes from a PR campaign.

A most common misconception about PR is that it's just publicity. This is far from the truth. Publicity is merely getting the word out. PR is a multifaceted approach to changing the way the public thinks about, feels about, and reacts to a certain company, person, service, or product, by a third-party affirmation. This is also the reason public relations is not advertising. Advertising is a controlled message – planned, purchased, and placed by a company to speak directly to the public. The results of PR are often more credible to the public because the message has been created and shared by an unbiased source.

Another misconception is that a public relations program is a luxury, something very expensive, excessive, and difficult to manage. On the contrary, a PR campaign launched within a small business is easily supervised and fun to implement. With the proper planning, the correct tools at your disposal, and a great deal of persistence, any small business can reap the rewards.

If done right, public relations can help your company do many things:

Establish a premium brand and image
Create high-profile awareness of the brand
Establish a consistent image across all marketing vehicles
Generate qualified sales leads and Web site traffic
Increase the ratio of sales to requests for information
Position your company's executives as industry experts

Branding

What exactly is a "brand"? A brand is a cultural, sensory image that surrounds your company or product and creates an indelible symbol in the minds of your customers; it's an assurance of quality and stability, making the selection worry-free for your customers; it's a significant source of competitive advantage and earning potential; and it's a promise of performance. Remember the foundation of every brand is perceived quality.

Branding is easy to understand if you break it down. The word "brand" is derived from "to burn" – picture the branding iron of the American West. The brand elicits emotions in consumers, affecting perceived reputation, quality, and service. It's not solely about the logo, the theme song, or the celebrity endorsement. It's about influencing the human experience through perception. Knowing this, why wouldn't a small business create a brand for itself?

Take, for example, the little round Sunkist orange. For the most part, its brand is the only thing that makes it different from every other orange in the produce aisle. Yet, consumers are happy to pay 15 cents more on every dollar for the Sunkist orange, primarily because consumers perceive it to be fresher, sweeter, and juicier than its competitors. Here, and in many other instances, brand equity is hugely valuable.

So what does this mean for your small business? The earlier you begin building a brand, the easier it will be and the less it will cost. Start now by scrutinizing your current brands (the name of your company and its products or services). Ask your current customers why they purchased from you, and what feelings your company evokes in them. Since it's the emotion that sells, the better you can understand the emotional basis for your customer's relationship with your brand, the better you can use it to strengthen bonds.

Getting Started

Even though it's vital to your business' welfare, don't enter into a public relations campaign too lightly. Since public relations isn't as clearly and quickly measurable as other programs in a company, it's crucial that the marketing communications manager fully understands what PR can and can't do, and be able to communicate this to upper management. A communications department is not an isolated branch of the business; a well-executed campaign includes participation from all sides.

To determine which path your small business should take, start from the finish: Identify your company's goals; isolate those vehicles that work toward those goals; and allocate funds and resources accordingly. Integrating multiple vehicles will make each vehicle work harder and is more cost effective. Integration lowers the true cost of selling

overall.

©RMR & Associates, Inc.

As you can see from the tactical implementation triangle, the most expensive way to sell your company is one-on-one sales calls. The most recent estimate is that one sales call costs $500. On the other hand, public relations can reach far more people at a much lower "cost per thousand." A good public relations campaign can result in articles in several different newspapers and publications and reach millions of people. The other benefit of using some of the broader-reaching vehicles, such as public relations and advertising, is that you can get your company name in front of a prospect before the one-on-one sales call and increase the chance of being effective. It is much easier to close a sale if the prospect has already heard of your company. The advantage of using an integrated approach is that you can combine these vehicles based on your needs, your budget, your time frame, and other variables to get the most effective program for your company.

All CFOs see is the bottom line on the balance sheet; they don't see the stellar relationships with key media, the heightened image and awareness, the increase in market share, and the improved reputation.

Public relations is most important, and therefore, should be better funded, for companies with a high FUD factor. FUD stands for fear, uncertainty, and doubt – an aspect of business that will influence how you approach a communications program. The media, as well as the public, experience FUD when introduced to a new company, product, or service. Technology is one of those industries that benefit from PR over advertising because of the general uncertainty about the products in the market. PR carries more weight in those markets because of its ability to facilitate third-party credibility. Companies with a pricier product also gain more return from public relations because the public is more likely to purchase a big-ticket item from a company that has been validated by the press.

To help the public overcome their FUD, small businesses must use public relations to position themselves as dependable, quality organizations with staying power and growth potential. Outreach must be consistent; messages must be controlled; and news must include growth-oriented information. Once the public is assured that your company is not a fly-by-night business, they'll feel comfortable buying from you.

It's always wise to assess your company's budgetary guidelines and constraints before making any program commitments. Even if you choose to perform most of the public relations functions in-house, you should allocate a budget for collateral and other materials, phone, fax, postage, and travel. Most companies, regardless of size, spend between 1 percent and 20 percent of total revenue on their communications program, depending on their offerings. Small businesses often spend between 5 percent and 10 percent of their total revenue on public relations. Many smaller companies decide to keep their functions in-house to reduce costs, only to realize they're spending more on those resources than agencies already have at their disposal. Agencies can work more efficiently by leveraging the existing relationships they have with the editorial community.

Goal Setting

Setting goals is a task many small businesses do annually. However, setting corporate goals doesn't always take into account integrating corporate messaging with the company's communications plan. First determine the company's goals for the upcoming year:

Initially introduce your company or a new product into the market?
Increase sales or market share?
Increase name, product, service recognition?
Improve your company's (its executives') reputation?

Once the company's goals are established, the PR team needs to align their efforts with the company's current focus. Public relations campaigns, while ongoing and consistent, do take on short-term, project-style features when news is in the pipeline. In the goal-setting stage, it is important to lay out your expected results for the marketing team, so they can strive to meet your goals. You will revisit these initial projections at the end of the campaign to measure how well your goals were reached through public relations efforts.

To attain measurable results, it is best to write out your goals at the beginning of the campaign. Having something concrete by which to measure your achievements will enable you to judge the effectiveness or success of the public relations program. This goal-setting stage should include evaluating the number of briefings you expect to be set, selecting the top five publications in which you want to get placements, and determining whether getting a cover story is a must-have. If you are introducing a new product, you should establish the number of product reviews you expect to see. If you are trying to raise awareness of your company and increase your name recognition, determine how you expect to measure those somewhat intangible results. Do you expect to have editors refer to you in articles, and conference coordinators to call you to speak at local or industry events? These goals should be realistic. Don't go into a project demanding a cover story in an industry-renowned publication, only to realize after the campaign is completed that the news wasn't that exciting. Once you determine your goals, you can choose those vehicles that will help fulfill them.

Research, Planning, and Preparation

You must complete numerous activities before embarking on a public relations campaign, including market research and competitive analysis. Before choosing your public relations vehicles, you should determine whether your goal is to better position yourself against other products, other markets, or other companies. If you want to conduct a full-blown market research program, I recommend you hire a marketing firm to conduct these activities for you before your PR campaign, since they can be very complex and time-consuming.

The second step is identifying your company spokesperson(s). Ideally, your spokesperson should be the highest-ranking executive possible, and he or she should have the expertise to handle the toughest questions. Your spokesperson should be the "voice of the company" in articles, on talk shows, and at conferences; however, when members of the media call the company directly (and this will happen more and more as you become a reliable resource for editors), the calls should be directed to the marketing communications manager, not the spokesperson, so the manager can prepare the spokesperson for responding to the nature of the call.

Next, develop a list of key media outlets. This "core list" of media targets is the skeleton of your media relations program. Savvy practitioners realize that 20 percent of the individuals in a market will influence the other 80 percent. You should identify groups of influential publications, including local and national print, broadcast, and online media outlets in those markets and trade categories that reach and influence your publics. And don't forget industry analysts, as well. Your extended list should include name, title, e-mail, and mailing addresses (mailing address and street address may be different), and phone and fax numbers. Other essential information should include preferred method of material receipt and deadlines (both day and time).

Each of the media outlets has a schedule of topics they plan to write on in upcoming issues, called an editorial calendar. Authored article opportunities, speaking opportunities, and award nominations are also on a schedule and have their own calendars. If you have time, select those articles within all the target outlets that your spokesperson is qualified to comment on, as well as all the authored article and award opportunities you'd like to apply for, and create your own opportunities spreadsheet. Cultivating long-term relationships with these editors can lead to articles that educate your target market, while at the same time educating the publications' readers.

Once you've determined your target audience and your spokesperson, you need to identify who in your organization will be conducting your outreach. This is where a public relations or media relations agency is beneficial, but if you have staff members who meet the following criteria, they'll do just fine.

Who in your company are your biggest cheerleaders?
Who has the best attitude?
Who are the most dedicated and persistent in their positions?
And most important, who can look rejection in the eye, time after time, day after day, and still come out fighting for your company's cause?

If you're lucky enough to have one or two of these dynamos in your organization, congratulations! You have now pinpointed your media relations team, and you're ready to prepare your arsenal of media relations supplies.

Media kits help you get most of your relevant information out in one neat package, and, in turn, help editors do their jobs more effectively. Anything that makes an editor's job easier increases your opportunities for exposure. Build your kit to ensure it's a functional and accurate presentation of your company's product and services. A media kit serves as an introductory piece to editors, analysts, investors, and partners. A comprehensive kit includes the following:

Recent press releases
Company background information
Biographies of spokespeople (You may want to include a headshot if the spokesperson is speaking at a tradeshow where the kit is being distributed.)
Case histories, testimonials, customer quotes
Article reprints
Product or service materials
FAQ or fact sheet
Customer or reference list
PowerPoint presentation snippets (once again, if a representative from the company is speaking at a tradeshow where the kit is being distributed)
Business card of the primary communications contact at your company. (This is very important for a number of reasons, not the least of which is media accessibility.)

As a rule, the contents of a media kit are more important than the format you present them in, but you want to ensure that the whole package accurately represents the culture of your company. A high-end, full-color, glossy folder will make your business look successful and well-established, but you don't want to blow your entire budget on printing (and reporters know you're bluffing if your kit is snazzier than Microsoft's). On the other hand, if you package your materials in a taped-up manila folder, you also send the wrong signal. Despite the emphasis on a "paperless environment," many editors still prefer a hard-copy media kit to electronic documents.

You should have enough media kits to send to each of your most important editorial contacts, and even more if you plan to exhibit or speak at conferences or tradeshows. It is a good rule of thumb to also reproduce the media kit components on your Web site.

Ready for Take-Off: PR Vehicles

On any journey, choosing the right vehicle determines when, and if, you'll reach your destination. The public relations journey is no different. For each type of journey, an array of vehicles is ready to deliver you there. Planning is key. Different combinations of vehicles can accomplish different things. Depending on your goals and your budget, you may want to use some vehicles more often, some less often, and some not at all. Review the descriptions, uses, and outcomes of the vehicles below to see which ones are best suited for your business.

Press Releases

Press releases are the most efficient way to communicate your news to the press, and a great way to disseminate your message exactly the way you want. A word of caution: Make sure your news is worthy before launching into the release writing and distribution process. Fluffy news only wastes your time, as well as that of the reporters you're sending it to, making your company look less credible in the eyes of the publication. Remember the editor's WIIFM rule:

What's In It For Me? If an editor looks at the headline of your press release and asks himself, "Why should I care?" it's not a newsworthy topic. Keep in mind that you should know your audience before you distribute your news to them. Not every publication and writer should get every one of your press releases. Determine who should be on your distribution list based on the type of news you are announcing. Product review editors should get new product announcements. New hires or new office space announcements should go only to editors at your local paper.

It also helps to write your releases in the style editors are used to – the inverted pyramid. Put the most important information in the first paragraph, and use the following paragraphs to fill in the details. If a reporter is getting 200 press releases every day, you want to make sure yours cuts through the clutter and captures him in the first paragraph. The golden rule of press releases is the shorter the better. You want to make sure that if the reporter has time to read only your first paragraph, he'll get your news.

There are many ways to distribute press releases. If you do it in-house (the most cost-effective, yet time-consuming method), make sure you send them the way your editors and analysts most prefer – mail, fax, e-mail, or courier. If you decide to use a newswire distribution service, research your options, and find the service that best reaches your intended markets for the lowest price. You may have to supplement your distribution through in-house methods anyway, depending on your market. Hint: Send your releases to your current and prospective customers, too!

Media Relations

This vehicle is not an option – it's a requirement! Media relations is proactive, consistent contact with editors in your market space. This is sometimes considered the most difficult public relations vehicle to integrate into a small business' communications plan, as it requires steadfast contact with the media. Media relations is a process that works only when it's constant and carefully crafted. This makes it challenging if a small business tries to keep their marketing efforts in-house because media relations demands the attention of one or two dedicated marketing professionals who have the time and energy to constantly funnel news to the press and keep them up-to-date on the company's latest announcements. However, media relations is also the most rewarding public relations vehicle, as it often leads to your best placements. Developing strong relationships with the reporters and editors who focus on your industry will result in quality articles.

Media relations is by far most difficult in the beginning of the program. Reporters experience fear, uncertainty, and doubt (FUD) when dealing with smaller, lesser-known companies with new, unproven products and services. Because of this uncertainty, it's harder to cut through the clutter, so it's important to be honest, helpful, and patient with the media. There is one advantage to reporters when dealing with small businesses: easier, quicker access to high-level executives.

The Internet has changed the dynamics of media relations. E-mail gets you right into a reporter's office, straight to the desktop, but your message can be deleted as quickly as it was opened. Don't spam, and don't send unsolicited e-mails. E-mail can cut press release distribution costs and reach those media outlets that wire services miss, but you should let reporters know why you're contacting them, and offer them an out if they're not interested in receiving more information from you. Courtesy goes a long way with reporters; don't take easy access for granted.

Although you want to contact reporters while they're working on an article relevant to your business, missed opportunities can still become future opportunities. For example, if you see an article that's written about one of your competitors or a trend story you think you should have been included in, you can use this moment to turn your company into a source. Call the reporter to tell him you saw his article, and because your company is very heavily involved in that market you'd like to tell him a little bit about what you're doing. After all, the reporter's primary function, like yours, is to inform the marketplace. A similar concept is latching on to a current event. For example, if your company manufactures security equipment, and the latest news in your community is focused on high school robberies, you can call your local print and broadcast media and offer your spokesperson's expertise for inclusion in a related piece.

Media relations also complements other vehicles. For instance, when you drop a press release, you should always follow up with a phone call or e-mail to explain to the reporter why this news should matter to him or her. As I mentioned before, reporters and editors get deluged with releases. You need to help them focus on your news.

(Note: Some smaller companies I've worked with have tried hiring a full-time person to be the media relations component, but found them being pulled into other aspects of the marketing effort, losing sight of the media relations goals. This is one vehicle that is best fulfilled by a team of media relations specialists at an agency. You'll be so thankful you outsourced this function.)

Media Training

Now that you've chosen your spokesperson, you must get started on media training right away. This should include identifying and memorizing the company's key message points, preparing the speaker for awkward questions, and teaching repetition and bridging techniques to ensure your spokesperson stays focused on the key message points. Ideally, your messages will be included, verbatim, in the interviewer's article. Many PR firms have media training capabilities that include video- and audio-taping to prepare for broadcast interviews. One thing to remember about media training is that you want to limit yourself to between three and five message points, and be sure to stick with them. Editors won't remember more than that. To be most effective, the message points should be phrased as benefits or differentiators and repeated as often as possible.

Briefings

Face-to-face briefings are a great way to build company recognition and trust with the media. Your spokesperson can tell reporters "the story behind the story," demonstrate the product or service your company provides, and comment on current topics within your industry. Use your meetings to develop long-term relationships with editors, rather than a one-time pitch and run.

Briefings can be scheduled while your media relations team is making calls on behalf of your latest news. Editors are seldom able to leave the newsroom, so offer to stop by their offices at lunch, or just after deadlines close, with food. Since time is limited, don't waste it. Take a media kit, your strongest messages, and solid insight into the writer's beat for best results.

Speaking Engagements

Arranging for experts in your company to speak at industry conferences, tradeshows, association meetings, seminars, or other forums allows direct contact with those decision-makers within your peer, customer, and vertical market groups. But remember these are not self-promotional excursions. You really want to make sure you're speaking to the audience and giving them information they can use, not merely plugging your product or service. Address the needs of the audience with relevant information.

Tradeshows

If you've decided to make a large financial and time commitment by exhibiting at a tradeshow, break through the clutter of all those competitors by pre-briefing attending editors with your announcements before the show. This not only gets you more attention; it actually causes editors to specifically search for your booth. Save some information for the show itself, however, so you have a reason to meet with the press again. You should also leave your briefing materials in pressrooms and information kiosks and post them online through the organizer of the show.

Case Histories

Effective case histories are stories written in a "problem, solution, results" format, showing your target audience how customers benefited from using your product or service. By showing how your company solved a real-life customer problem, you not only add credibility to your message, but you also help editors flesh out stories by providing them additional sources. Make sure you get approval before you use one of your customers as a reference. Also, try to get them on board with the message points you most want to stress. It's great publicity for their company too, so it's a two-way street. You can get a lot of mileage from case histories: Your salespeople can take them on calls or pitches, and you can include them in your advertising campaign.

Awards

Corporate and product awards add credibility to your organization and message, but they rarely "just happen" on their own. Learn about the nomination process by speaking with the review boards, past winners, and judges. The time spent researching and applying for awards can be the most productive time you ever spend because you uncover more in-depth information about your business. Your clients and customers will also like buying from a "winner."

Authored Articles

These bylined articles help position you and your company as authorities in your market space. They don't necessarily have to be written by the individuals at your organization. Good PR agencies work with freelancers who ghost-write articles on behalf of their clients. So if an opportunity arises where an editor is looking for an authored article, your expert doesn't have to take the time to write it on his or her own. And once the article is written, you can use it as a sales tool by sending reprints to your current and potential customers. Frequently, the articles can be leveraged as speaking topics, as well.

Community Relations

If your company's budget and resources can support it, community relations is a fun and effective way to connect with your customers, while strengthening the image and reputation of the business. By spearheading or sponsoring community events, your company can demonstrate its commitment to providing for the neighborhood and the people in it. If your small business is consumer-focused, hand out samples of your product at the event. If your company attracts business customers, donate your product or service to a school, community center, or non-profit organization. These feel-good sponsorships are great fodder for other PR vehicles: press releases, case histories, and campaign award nominations.

Web Site

Even if you don't plan to sell anything online, you cannot afford to disregard the power of the Internet. Gone are the days when your customers pull out the Yellow Pages or dial directory assistance. With the Internet, you can welcome your customers and potential customers into your world with just a few clicks. Make sure your site has the same look and feel, and similar content, as your other marketing materials, and that it's easy to navigate. Some important links or pages your site should contain include:

Company background
Description of products and services
Contacts (who's who and what they do)
Media room
Testimonials
FAQs

All PR vehicles serve a purpose, but some vehicles are more important to small businesses than others. My experience tells me that the three most essential PR vehicles are media relations, speaking engagements, and authored articles. These three allow you to advance your position in your industry, help you reach your target audiences, and attract customers more efficiently.

Small businesses have an advantage over large corporations when it comes to making the most of current events and trends. There are fewer approvals to get when the marketing department wants to launch a new campaign. Smaller companies have a better focus on their market segment. Because small businesses have that one-to-one interaction with a customer base, they understand problems and pains better.

Public relations success is spelled with three P's: persistence, perseverance, and propensity for action. No PR plan, no matter how well-thought or well-funded, will work if the people executing the program aren't in it 100 percent. Relations with the media take time to cultivate and may not always bring the desired results, but it's crucial to continue.

Weekly meetings are also vital to your program. Rally the troops over bagels and coffee, and invite them to share ideas, challenges, and successes from the previous week. These meetings also give you a chance to communicate goings-on in other departments, especially those that have an impact on marketing activities (new product developments, new hires, changes in service offerings).

Corporate Identity – Look and Feel of Your Business

A corporate identity package will give your small business a big-business image and is significant in the branding process. You can get a lot of mileage from a well-designed identity package that accurately represents your company's offerings. Any good marketing or advertising agency can create a logo and help you choose colors that you'll carry through your entire communications campaign, from business cards and letterhead to direct mail to your ad campaign (dream big!). Even if your budget isn't as big as your dreams, you'll be able to develop some of these pieces for relatively low cost:

Corporate logo
Corporate brochure
Letterhead and envelopes
Mailing labels
Business cards

Results

Just as you begin with research, you should end with research. No public relations campaign is over until you figure out whether, and how, you've met your goals. Why is the "how" important? Because if the vehicles you've chosen aren't working, you should try something else.

The first "how" is to conduct another round of market research to determine whether your target audience was affected by your communications and outreach efforts. Are consumers more aware of your company name and product?

Has there been an increase in demand for your product or service? Is your Web site getting more traffic and inquiries? The marketing agency you used before launching the PR campaign can help you with the follow-up market research. Tracking results can include tangible figures, such as the number of placements, hits, and speaking engagements, and hard numbers, such as advertising equivalencies – a dollar figure that identifies what the placement would have been worth if you had had to buy the equivalent ad space. Measurable results can also include intangibles, such as evaluating an article to determine the tone (positive or negative) and whether your key message points were cited. An article that highlights your company and product in a positive light should be worth much more than one that inaccurately portrays who you are and what you do.

With the help of a media clipping service, you can evaluate media relations in-house. For a monthly fee and per-clip charge, media clipping services scan print, broadcast, and online media outlets for mentions of your company, and provide them to you. This is the best way to track where you're getting coverage, and it's nearly impossible to do it on your own – you'd have to subscribe to and read every publication you sent your releases to.

To evaluate your media efforts, choose your qualifiers based on your goals, for instance, "relevant media outlet?", "accurate message?" or "proximate to press release drop?" What good is an article in *Road & Track* if your product is a sofa bed? Once your qualifiers are in place, use them to rate each placement. When you're finished, find your success percentage by dividing the number of on-target placements with the number of overall placements. Now that's measuring public relations success one article at a time.

Beyond the Campaign: Consistency Is Key

Once you've established and initiated your public relations program, you need to remember that everything your company does, and every word your employees speak on behalf of the company, is a reflection of the business. Make sure your automated voicemail system works well, is easy to navigate, and reflects your company's culture. If you have a receptionist, that person should be trained in customer service, as he or she is the first impression your customers and prospects encounter. Suggest to your staff that they don't discuss internal business in public (especially problems) and that they wear their logo attire to events, and with pride. Encourage them not to speak to the media directly, but to point the media in the direction of the spokesperson, who has completed media training. Remember that perception is reality, and your employees are ambassadors of your business. And while the media contact should be limited to the spokesperson, be sure the entire company knows the messaging and branding and has a comprehensive understanding of where the company is going.

The Challenges

Time is certainly a challenge every business faces, and small businesses feel the crunch even more profoundly. It's easy to lose focus and momentum when other tasks are looming over you and your department, but remember that PR is an ongoing activity, and to abandon it only hurts your company. If you decide to keep your public relations in-house, you must be able to dedicate one or two full-time staff members to promoting your company. A safe schedule for public relations activity is one day a week (or four days out of the month). This doesn't have to mean you should be calling editors once a week to harass them with each little news tidbit. But it does mean you designate someone in your company to review your company's marketing communications efforts to make sure a consistent message is being delivered to the media, so your company remains visible. This allows you to be constant with your outreach, yet doesn't overtake your other responsibilities (or those of your staff).

Budget is also always a challenge, but if you determine your budget early in the program and set realistic expectations, you can construct a public relations campaign that has the same impact as those on a larger scale.

No Magic, No Secret Code

If all this direction is getting you lost, you may want to work with an agency. Don't feel intimidated by the thought of hiring an agency to implement your PR campaign; agencies and their well-trained professionals act as an extension to your in-house team and can save you time and frustration.

One of the best ways to choose an agency is through a referral. Talk to other small business owners in your area to see who they've used or heard of. If that isn't helpful, contact the Council of Public Relations Firms at www.prfirms.org. Through its site, you can select a PR firm based on location, size, disciplines, and other factors. Many of the firms listed there have been audited by the Council and have very good reputations. When reviewing agencies, remember to ask about other clients (Will your small company get lost in the crowd of larger clients?), team composition (Who exactly will you be working with?), and billing methods (project versus retainer billing).

Remember that someone in your company must be the main contact for your agency. Although your agency team will help you identify and implement your goals, messages, and vehicles, don't rely on them to run the campaign for you. Weekly meetings are a must, and in them, be prepared to talk about progress, challenges, and new ideas (much as you would if you constructed a team in-house). Nothing enhances a client-agency relationship like outstanding communication.

Public relations has no secret code and no strange ingredients, but it can do magic for your small business. It's also an excellent way to bring your company's departments together, stay connected with your customers, and make a name for yourself in your community and industry. With some planning, persistence, and a little luck, your business can reap the reward of public relations.

Christopher P.A. Komisarjevsky, Burson-Marsteller Worldwide, President & Chief Executive Officer

The CEO as Chief Communications Officer

An important challenge for the public relations industry is helping people understand that a company's chief executive is actually the company's chief communications officer. No one else in the company has the responsibility the chief executive has; no one has the platform the chief executive holds; and most important, no one has the understanding of the goals and ultimate vision of the company like the chief executive.

From the public's perspective, the chief executive symbolizes the company, speaks for the company, and is seen as possessing the company's brand values. A strong CEO – delivering the right messages – makes an enormous difference in the valuation of a company, while inaction or missteps can have dire, instantaneous consequences.

We recommend that CEOs take the following steps to maximize their effectiveness:

Set an agenda and create a vision for the future; then become the architect of the company's vision and values. If successful, they will be better able to recruit and retain the best talent that they need to execute their agenda and gain respect nationally and internationally.

Build a strong senior management team, and keep team members acting in unison.

Measure – and manage – what matters: quality service and products, the level of stock recommendations, and "best-in-class" and "employer-of-choice" status.

Listen carefully to word of mouth and online activity – about their company and about themselves.

Communicate regularly and proactively with internal and external audiences, using all appropriate channels and methods of communication.

Listen to customers, clients, employees, financial community members, and shareholders, so that they meet expectations.

Know the type of information that shareholders need, and deliver it personally.

Keep pace with change, and use technology to their competitive advantage, so they can operate on a global scale, accelerate change and decision-making, and be recognized as forward-thinking, innovative leaders.

At a *Chief Executive* magazine CEO roundtable, Dana Mead of Tenneco asked other CEOs, "How many of you have talked to institutional investors about your company, spending time on leadership development, employee training or environmental performance?" Not many had, as it turned out. CEOs who make the time to communicate with stakeholders can gain a competitive advantage; those who do not run the risk of letting others manage their fate.

The chief executive's visibility and ability to articulate his or her company's unique niche in the market are essential to shaping public perception. When people look at a company and to the chief executive, they look at the chief executive's values, and then they wait to see if those values and beliefs are reflected in production processes, employee treatment, customer relations, and other company operations and practices.

Communications Capital™

All business professionals know that the value of a corporation is built upon tangible assets – plants and machinery – and intangible assets, or its intellectual capital. In fact, in tomorrow's business environment, intangible assets will grow significantly in importance. Although opinions differ on how to categorize intangibles, we divide them into four categories:

Market Capital: The intelligence that goes into creating and developing new products and services, not the physical product itself. It also includes intangible attributes closely related to products, such as trademarks, patents, brand reputation, corporate reputation, and other marketing materials.

Human Capital: The knowledge, skills, and competencies that managers and employees possess.

Structural Capital: Any type of knowledge or innovation that has an impact on IT platforms, internal processes, manufacturing, or distribution.

Relationship Capital: The company's relationships with its customers and other stakeholders, including investors, government agencies, and communities.

Historically, the value of intangibles was considered relatively modest compared with financial assets, such as buildings, equipment, and inventory. But we now know that this is not the case.

Forbes ASAP put it best: "Today, when intangible assets can make up a huge portion of a company's value, and when that value is remeasured every business day by stock market analysts and traders, our current system of financial measurement has become increasingly disconnected from what appears to be truly valuable in the new economy." It is estimated today that intangible assets are three times greater in value than tangible assets. For example, Microsoft has very little in the way of tangible assets, but it is greatly respected by the entire marketplace for its intangible assets and intellectual capital.

To quote Leif Edvinsson of Scandia Insurance, whom many consider to be "the father of intellectual capital," "The intellectual capital of nations is the new wealth of nations."

Communications Capital is the strategic use of communications to leverage a company's intellectual capital, and as a result gain even more value – higher valuations – than might otherwise have been possible. It encompasses the proper review, assessment, packaging, and communication of intangible assets, and can mean the difference between success and failure. At our firm, we believe Communications Capital is a Fifth Capital – an intangible asset category that infuses the other four (Market, Human, Structural, and Relationship Capital) and enables them to resonate in the marketplace.

On the upside, the benefits of Communications Capital, of leveraging and communicating intangibles, are wide-ranging:

Positive analyst recommendations
Increased investor demand
A higher number of repeat customers
Premium pricing
A larger number of committed employees
A broader talent pool
Motivated partners
Higher quality vendors

Because these benefits contribute to a company's bottom line in a very real way, Communications Capital is easily redeemed for hard currency.

Our firm has begun to explore the impact of communications on influential business people – CEOs, senior executives, financial analysts, government officials' and journalists. Our results show companies that communicate their strategy command a higher MVA (market value added) and EVA (economic value added) than other firms. Investors are also more likely to put a higher value on the intangible assets of a firm that has effective communications.

Building Communications Capital is a key CEO responsibility. To perform his or her job to the fullest, CEOs need the best that communications can bring. Failing to accept this challenge can create precipitous gaps between a company's actual worth and its perceived value among key stakeholders. These gaps can seriously damage a company's reputation, making it less likely that audiences will invest in the company, purchase its products or services, or look upon it favorably as an employer or as a joint-venture or strategic-alliance partner.

We recommend a multistep, integrated process for reviewing, assessing, packaging, and communicating intangible assets. Companies wishing to develop strong Communications Capital need to develop communications processes with the following features:

Right leadership: Support from a company's top leadership. The CEO must be involved.

Right resources: The capacity, infrastructure, and staff to deliver the correct amount of intangible information in a timely manner.

Right strategy: An emphasis on the company's vision and strategy.

Right relationships: The ability to develop a dialogue with key stakeholder groups and build relationships over time.

Right information: Disclosure of relevant intangible-asset information with stakeholders in a straightforward manner.
Right feedback: Shifting dialogue from one-way to two-way, always respecting different opinions and measuring progress on key communications goals.

Rich Jernstedt, Golin/Harris International, Chief Executive Officer

---

The Five Cs of Successful Branding

Public relations adds context, texture, emotion, and definition to a brand, so the audience – whether it's a customer, an employee, or a shareholder – can develop the trust that needs to exist with the brand. It is based on having enough information to make a choice, an individual choice, about how one feels about this brand. It's all about accessing information from a credible source, so an individual can make a decision about how to feel about a brand.

The greatest brands in the world achieved the status by following what our firm calls the Five C's of Successful Branding.

First of all, one has to have a compelling proposition that's high-impact and relevant. It has to mean something of importance.

The second element in building a successful brand is to be sure there is some way of distinguishing between it and other brands that may compete for the same or similar positioning. In other words, there is a clear and distinctive position that is yours alone. If you stand for something, you stand out. By understanding what is truly unique about your organization, or brand, and staying focused on it, you define and then own the position. You can't be all things to all people, so narrow the focus appropriately. If you narrow your focus, you expand your impact.

The third C is that there must be consistent delivery of the brand promise. It can be trusted and relied upon every day and in every place. Communicate what you are about…and communicate it again. It requires some discipline, of course, and maybe some creativity to find different ways to communicate the same promise.

The fourth is a connection with the stakeholders. More simply put, there has to be a meaningful and emotional bond. Care about what they care about.

And fifth is a commitment to leadership and innovation. Your brand will be important in an ever-changing environment and can be trusted today and tomorrow. It means meeting or exceeding the expectations of your key audiences. And it means setting the bar for your competition. Ironically, it may mean joining with your competition to solve large issues. It certainly means changing as necessary, to continually strive for excellence in everything the brand means.

Jay Conrad Levinson, Best Selling Author

What Is Guerrilla Marketing

Guerrilla marketing is pursuing conventional goals using unconventional means.

Guerrilla marketing begins with an idea for how to generate profits for a business and becomes a circle when that business has the blessed patronage of repeat and referral customers. I used to compare guerrilla marketing with textbook marketing, but guerrilla marketing is becoming textbook marketing. In a few years it will be traditional marketing. It seems the only way to fly.

There are 18 strategies that differentiate guerrilla marketing from what is currently considered traditional marketing:

Invest Time, Not Money

Traditional marketing says that a marketer's primary investments should be money. With guerrilla marketing the primary investments should be time, energy, and imagination. If marketers are willing to invest enough time, energy, and imagination, they don't have to invest as much money.

I know people who spend $30 a month doing guerrilla marketing. They post signs on bulletin boards, maybe on college campuses, or maybe in communities where a lot of people gather around bulletin boards. Many of these marketers use email. They get the names of people from user groups, so they know that these people are interested in this particular topic. And email is free, so they can conduct much of their marketing that way. They might write articles that get posted on other companies' Web sites. That takes time, energy, and imagination, but it does not take money. So it's very possible to market successfully for $50 to $100 a month. Naturally, the more companies invest, the more profits they'll make—if they're going about everything else right.

Measure Performance by Profitability

Traditional marketing measures its performance by sales or by store traffic, while guerrilla marketing focuses on profits. Anybody can achieve high sales, but it takes talent to generate ever-increasing profit.

One reason people go into business is to give themselves joy in life and to provide balance in their lives, but the main reason is to earn a profit. Too many people lose sight of that and focus only on sales, thinking that, "The more people I get into my store or the more people I get responding to my offer, the more money I'll make." Sometimes they'll get a lot of people into their stores and they'll make a lot of sales. But they're not making much money, because they're not making a lot of money on each sale and the cost of doing business is subtracting even more. That's why guerrillas find it extremely important to focus only on profits, because that's ultimately how executives build their businesses.

Know the Tools

Traditional marketing seems to intimidate a lot of people, because it's enshrouded by mystique. People aren't quite sure what marketing is. They're not sure if it includes sales and they're not certain if advertising really is marketing. Guerrilla marketers feel no sense of intimidation and to them there is no mystique about marketing.

Spend Small

Traditional marketing has always been geared to big businesses with big bankrolls. Although big businesses and Fortune 500 companies buy boxes of guerrilla marketing books at a time, the reality is that guerrilla marketing is geared to small businesses, to the small-business owner with big dreams but a tiny bank account.

Eliminate Guesswork

Traditional marketing has always been based on experience and judgments—it's a fancy way of guesswork. Guerrillas cannot afford to make wrong guesses. So as much as possible guerrilla marketing is based on psychology. For example, guerrilla marketers know that 90 percent of purchase decisions are made in the unconscious mind, and they know that a slam-dunk manner of accessing the human unconscious mind is through repetition.

Maintain Focus

Traditional marketing says that companies should grow their businesses large and then diversify into different fields and different services. Guerrilla marketing says that companies will probably get in trouble if they do that; the ability to maintain focus will lead to a company's success much more than its concept of diversifying.

Grow Geometrically

Traditional marketing has always said that companies should add new customers one at a time. That's an expensive way to grow: arithmetically. Guerrilla marketing tries to grow companies geometrically, enlarging the size of each transaction and having more transactions with each customer. This approach taps the enormous referral power of a company's existing customers, because it costs so much less to sell to an existing customer. While the company is doing that it's also adding new customers. If a company is growing geometrically it's hard to not turn a profit and to not stay in business successfully.

The Follow-Up

Follow-up is a big issue, because so few people do it. Traditional marketing seems to have aimed at making the sale, period, while guerrilla marketing is big on follow-up. Guerrilla marketers say, "You have to make a sale and then follow up with that customer." In the United States nearly 70 percent of lost business is lost due to apathy after the sale, not to poor service or shabby quality. It's lost due to customers being ignored after the purchase. That's why guerrillas follow up with all of their customers and stay in touch with customers once they become customers. Marketers can't wait for customers to come to them; they have to constantly be proactive and be in touch with customers, any way they can—post cards, mailings, email, faxes, telephone calls, anything—as long as the marketers are telling customers that they're important.

Create Partnerships

Traditional marketing says to scan the horizon for the competition and see what companies to obliterate; guerrilla marketing says to forget the competition and scan the horizon for those businesses with which the firm might cooperate. The reason is simple: Marketing partners lower the total marketing costs and the increase the reach of both partners. So cooperation, not competition, is the name of the game for guerrillas.

Use "You" Marketing

Traditional marketing is "me" marketing. A prospect goes to a company's Web site and it says, "Let me tell you about me; let me tell you why my company is so big, why my company is so wonderful." Guerrilla marketing is "you" marketing. It says, "Here's how you can benefit from trying this new service; here's how your life could be made better if you try this new product. It's all about you and not about me." Guerrilla marketing is always oriented to the customer, not the company, because people are interested in themselves more than in any company.

Help Customers Succeed

Traditional marketers have always been interested in taking and in seeing how much money they can get from each of their customers. Guerrilla marketing is all about giving. Guerrilla marketers think about what can they do to help their customers succeed at their goals, because the wider the conduit through which a company's generosity flows, the wider the conduits will be when the profits flow back.

Use Marketing Combinations

Traditional marketing would have people believe that just advertising works or that just having a Web site works, or that just direct mail works; guerrilla marketing says that's just not true. It's folly to believe that. Advertising doesn't work alone anymore, neither does having a Web site, and certainly direct mail doesn't work alone. So what does work? The only thing that works these days is marketing combinations, running advertising *and* having a Web site *and* doing direct mail. All three will help each other work. The days of single-weapon marketing have been relegated to the past; we're living in a time in which only marketing combinations work. It makes me sad to see so many wonderful Web sites out there that there's no way to know about unless someone happens upon them. If those companies marketed their sites in other media, that marketing combination would make their Web sites successful.

Build Relationships

At the end of each month traditional marketers count up how much money they've brought in, while guerrilla marketers count up how many new relationships they've made. Guerrilla marketers know that relationships are vitally important, and the longer the relationships, the more sales they will eventually make and the more profits they will eventually earn. So guerrillas cherish every relationship they make.

Embrace Technology

Traditional marketing never really made an allowance for technology, primarily because technology was too complex, expensive, not quite powerful enough, and it was hard for the average small-business owner to understand. That has all changed. The biggest change in technology is that it has become easy to use. So guerrilla marketing requires that marketers be technocozy. If marketers are technophobic they should make an appointment with their technoshrinks, because technophobia is fatal these days. And technology is more inexpensive, more powerful, smaller, and far less complex than it used to be.

Target Individuals

Traditional marketing always aims its messages at groups, the larger the group the better. Guerrilla marketing aims its message at individuals, just a few individuals at a time; if it's going to be a group, the smaller the group the better.

Consider the Details

Traditional marketing only identifies the mass weapons of marketing like radio, television, magazines, newspapers, and the Internet. As a result, many other marketing tools get overlooked, such as the way a company's telephone is answered. That's an important part of marketing, because some of the most important people on earth, customers and prospects, call on companies. What happens in traditional marketing is that some of the marketing happens unintentionally, leaving at great risk whether the marketing will be good or bad. Guerrilla marketers are aware of all the details of marketing, including the attire worn by their companies' representatives and how their employees treat people on the telephone. Guerrilla marketing is always intentional and nothing is left to chance.

Gain Consent

Traditional marketing has always aimed to make the sale with the marketing. Because there is so much marketing going on today, it's hard to make a sale with one piece of marketing. So guerrilla marketing attempts to gain consent from prospects to receive a company's marketing material. Once a business has gained that consent, it markets only to those people. When a company does that, it's not wasting its money by mailing to or marketing to disinterested people.

Increase the Marketing Arsenal

Finally, traditional marketers have always had a limited arsenal. As I said, they usually go for radio, television, magazines, newspapers, direct mail, telemarketing, and Internet. Guerrilla marketing identifies 100 different marketing weapons and 62 of them are free. The idea of guerrilla marketing is to become aware of all 100 marketing weapons and to use as many as is feasible; to pay careful attention to those weapons and eliminate those that aren't working. Companies that use guerrilla marketing are going to find out that their marketing arsenal may consist of 20 different weapons, and of those 20 weapons maybe half of them are free. So the size of the arsenal of the guerrilla marketer is much larger than the arsenal for the traditional marketer.

Change Is in the Air

These 18 differences not only summarize the contrast between guerrilla marketing and traditional marketing, but also point to the way marketing is heading. Take the Internet as an example. Over the past few years the Internet has really begun to leave its infancy and become a pre-adolescent. People are beginning to learn how to use the Internet and that has made a major change in marketing.

The other big change is the idea that there is so much marketing coming down the pike that it's difficult for marketing to make its sale. That's why these days guerrillas go for consent from people and then market to those people.

There is so much marketing in so many forms: radio, television, magazines, newspapers, billboards, online banners, email. Because there is so much of it, almost all of it is interruption marketing. It's interrupting the person's day. Hardly anybody watches television with the idea of watching the commercials, therefore when the commercial comes on it's interrupting them. When people get an email about something they're not interested in they're just going to delete it, because it's interrupting their day and the flow of their lives.

There is so much interruption marketing right now that marketers need to do something to stand apart from it. The way to do that is to use some interruption marketing to get consent from people. Companies do that by offering prospects a free brochure or by directing them to a Web site; then they get prospects' consent to receive more marketing materials via email or via them requesting the free brochure. The majority will not give their consent, and companies don't mind, because that means they can save money by not marketing to those people anymore. But a small portion will give consent. Those people want to receive the marketing materials, they're interested in what the company has to say and what it has to offer. Once they've given a company their consent, its marketing budget gets much smaller. When a sale is made, it requires momentum to be established, and when someone gives consent, that begins the momentum.

One other change that has had and is having a dramatic effect on marketing is the low cost of television advertising, which has dropped significantly because of cable television, and the low cost of magazine advertising, because there are more regional additions of magazines. Those low costs of major media make it possible for every business to market in more arenas.

Those are ways that marketing has changed, but there's more to come. Technology is going to change marketing significantly. It's going to make almost all marketing far more interactive. Consumers will even be able to interact with television commercials. The more that consumers are allowed to be interactive, the more guerrilla marketing will flourish. Guerrilla marketing will change as technology changes. Guerrilla marketers do not resist change. In fact, they try to embrace change not for the sake of change but for the sake of improvement.

It's Just Human Nature

Technology will continue to change, but human beings will continue to be pretty much the same as they were a century ago. They still want a good value, they still want to be treated as individuals, they still like a smile, they like eye contact, they like people using their names. Consequently, although guerrilla marketers will embrace the technological changes that are pouring out of laboratories, they will always keep in mind that human nature has not changed much.

Marketers need to understand what's first and foremost on every human being's mind: the person himself or herself. People do not think about companies or products or services; they think about themselves. In the back of their minds whenever they read a marketing message is, "What's in it for me? What am I going to get out of it?" Although marketing has changed substantially in the past 100 years, especially the past 10 years, human nature really hasn't. The whole human race is selfish. Self-interest is at the basis of everything when they're reading marketing messages. Marketers must speak to the people not about their companies but about the people themselves.

This is one reason so many companies, even those with huge marketing budgets, aren't getting the marketing right. Another significant reason is that marketing and advertising agencies have always been the domain of young people and the market is not young people. The market is primarily older people. It's getting older and the advertising people are getting younger. The people who create advertising worship at the shrine of cleverness and cuteness. They're big on "me too"-ism and they try to copy other advertisers. This is a major mistake. The people who create marketing these days seem to be embarrassed that it's marketing. They don't want consumers to know that it's an ad that's running on television. They try to hide that with celebrity endorsements or special effects or wonderful music; as a result they create fabulous films that are ineffective advertising, ineffective marketing. Guerrilla marketing, on the other hand, is always going to be in vogue, because it's able to grow with the times while keeping in mind that people don't.

Attacking the Market

Once marketers understand the differences between traditional marketing and guerrilla marketing and take the time to acquire the traits necessary to be a successful guerrilla marketer, it's time to plan and implement their attack. This is a 10-step process.

Step One: Research

Before diving into a plan, guerrilla marketers must do their homework. They have to research their own markets to see what competitors are out there. They need to research their product to determine what the real benefits are, and talk to customers to find out what they perceive as the benefits. And they should research which benefits are most meaningful to both customers and prospects. Guerrillas have to research the media to see what media are available for their companies. For example, many marketers don't know the low cost of television these days. Businesses can be on prime-time television for $20 or less for one 30-second television commercial in almost any major market because of cable and satellite television.

Research also includes examining the competition, because many companies aim for the same customers and prospects. Guerrillas must research their industry to find trends and to see what are the newest things that organizations are able to offer to their customers.

Most important, guerrilla marketers research their customers to find out what makes them tick—what magazines they read, what newspapers they subscribe to, what TV shows they watch, where they go online, what tradeshows they go to, what is their family make up, what sports teams they follow. When marketers start learning about their customers, then they know what to look for in their prospects. Marketers have to conduct research into those prospects, because the prospects hopefully will become customers.

There are many ways to learn about customers. The best and the most inexpensive way is to prepare a customer questionnaire that asks a lot of questions of the customers about themselves. Be sure to have a paragraph at the top of the questionnaire that says, "We're sorry to be asking you so many questions, but the more we know about you the better service we can be to you." That makes sense to people, so they'll take the time to answer questions. Ask questions about what TV and radio shows they watch, ask questions about their families, their favorite sports teams, their kids' favorite activities at school. Marketers who learn about their customers in that detail can, for example, send a Thanksgiving Day card that says, "Happy Thanksgiving and congratulations on your daughter being named to the cheerleading squad," instead of sending a plain Christmas card like every other company. Guerrillas use the information they gain about customers to create really personalized marketing messages. And by gaining those insights into customers it's easier to find out where to find more people like them, people who match a target-customer profile.

Finally, guerrilla marketers must research the Internet. Markets are changing so rapidly that the only way to find out about what's happening is by researching the Internet.

If marketers do all that research—their market, their product, the media, their competition, their industry, their prospects and customers, the technology of the day, the benefits they offer, and the Internet—they're doing the right kind of research to get their marketing plan off to a fast start.

Step Two: List the Benefits

It's now necessary to write a list of the benefits the company offers. Put a star next to those benefits that are competitive advantages, because that's where marketers should really hang their marketing hats. It's necessary to be clear on the benefits and on the competitive advantages.

Step Three: Select the Weapons

Next, marketers must select the weapons that they're going to use. They may select a lot of weapons, but the amount should not be overwhelming, because it's necessary to take those weapons and put them in priority order and put a date next to each one of them. This creates a commitment to the date by which each weapon will be launched. And put a person's name with each weapon, because somebody's going to be in charge of launching that weapon—maybe the ad agency, maybe the marketer herself, maybe the director of marketing.

Step Four: Create a Plan

The next, crucial step is planning. Why? Why is a road map necessary to someone making a cross-country trip? And why are navigation aids necessary to people making long flights? They help propel them toward their goals. A marketing plan does the same thing. It lets marketers know what their goals are and then directs them toward those goals. Marketers who start without a plan will probably head off in the wrong direction and may lose sight of their goals as they continue on. A marketing plan serves as a road map to their goals. It forces marketers to focus on what their marketing should do.

It's also necessary for guerrillas to set milestones at the start of a campaign. It's important for marketers to quantify their goals in order to quantify how many and what kind of responses they want, what kind of profits they need, what kind of sales, and how fast turnover has to be. Marketers must quantify those things with milestones in writing. It's not enough to say, "We'll build our business this year." Instead marketers should say, "We will build our business to achieve an 11 percent growth in profits within the end of one year." That way they're much better equipped to keep track of how well they're doing. Marketers need to put their milestones in the form of specific numbers.

Although planning is vital, the final marketing plan should be brief. One of the reasons for the failure of businesses, especially small businesses, is either failure to start with a plan or having a plan that's so complicated it's hard to follow. A guerrilla marketing plan is only seven sentences long:

1) The first sentence tells the specific purpose of the marketing itself, and it ought to be a short sentence. This is the best way to start any marketing plan. Maybe the purpose is to get people to send for a free video, or to get them to visit a Web site or come to a store or call an 800 number.

2) The second sentence tells the benefits the marketing will stress to achieve the company's purpose. For example, if people don't buy this shampoo, they won't have good-looking hair. And it's important to stress the benefits in a short sentence, because marketers shouldn't put out all the benefits, just the main benefits.

3) The third sentence tells the target audience. Sometimes there may be more than one target audience, but again that's a short sentence. The target audience may be bigger when it's a large business that may be able to use even more marketing weapons and use them more heavily than a traditional guerrilla with a limited budget. Large companies can aim for a larger niche in the marketplace; they can't operate with small niches. They need larger niches, bigger chunks of humanity. Guerrillas with small businesses can operate successfully with a small niche; they have more warmth and personal contact.

4) The fourth sentence is the only long sentence, and should be written as a list. It enumerates the marketing weapons that the marketer plans use. The best approach is to start out

with a long list and try a lot of weapons and see which ones are proven in action.

5) The fifth sentence tells the company's niche in the marketplace, what it stands for. When people hear the name of a company, what's the first thing that enters their minds? That is the niche, and that should be stated in writing in the marketing plan.

6) The sixth sentence tells the firm's identity, its personality—not its image, because an image is something phony. An identity is what a company really is. All companies have a personality, and the best thing to do is put it in writing in the marketing plan. Then that personality will come shining through in all of the firm's other marketing materials.

7) The seventh sentence tells the marketing budget. Guerrillas should express their marketing budget as a percentage of their projected gross sales, not their previous year's sales, because then they're operating in the status quo. If they want to operate in growth mode they make it a percentage of their projected gross sales in the coming year.

The average American business invests 4 percent of gross sales in marketing. Fifty percent of companies go out of business within five years, so guerrilla marketers don't want to do things the way the average business does. Guerrillas don't try to do anything that average businesses do. They try to rise above the average, so they're willing to invest more than 4 percent of their projected gross sales in marketing. Ten percent is a good place to start. Once marketers get that 10 percent, they're building share of mind. As they build share of mind that percentage can drop, because total dollars will grow but the amount of money put into marketing can stay the same. As a result, the percent guerrilla marketers invest in marketing decreases each year, even though their profits increase.

But the marketing budget for a small business would be very different from that of a large firm. Although the percentage may be the same, the absolute dollar expenditure would be much larger on the part of a large company. Big businesses need to do that to support their overhead, but most guerrilla companies are lean machines and don't have as large an overhead.

That's all guerrilla marketers really need to get going with their plan. They can have 200 or 300 pages of documentation later on, but the marketing plan should start with a brief seven-sentence strategy. This is true whether the plan is for a small business or a huge conglomerate. Each one will have its own purpose. They'll each have their own specific benefits. Other than that, the marketing of big and small businesses is pretty much alike. In fact, Proctor & Gamble is as big and as sophisticated a marketing company as anyone will ever find, but its marketers use three-to five-sentence marketing plans to begin. They may have a lot of documentation later, but they start with simple plans that are easy to understand and easy to follow.

Step Five: Build a Calendar

Once the plan is written, it's time to make a guerrilla marketing calendar on which marketers should project out for one year what they're going to be doing month by month when it comes to marketing. The marketing calendar lists five things: the months of the year, the thrust of the marketing for each month, the media being used each month, how much money will be invested in marketing each month, and a grade for each month. The grades should be A, B, C, D or F, so that the second year's marketing calendar eliminates those months that only got C's, D's, or F's. Guerrillas only use those that get A's and B's. The third marketing calendar should have only things that got an A the year before.

One important thing to remember is to never cut back on marketing in a down cycle. This is a wonderful time to continue marketing and win over a lot of customers who ordinarily would not have known about the company. Marketers can only do this properly if they have a marketing calendar from the start that tells them when they are going to be doing their marketing, and based on the history of their businesses, they will know when the up periods and down periods are. It's a huge mistake to cut back during a down period.

Step Six: Find Fusion Partners

The next step is finding fusion-marketing partners. These are businesses that can share the marketing burden with a company; firms that have the same kind of standards, the same kind of prospects. *Business Week* calls it cooperative marketing, other people call it co-marketing, guerrillas call it fusion marketing. Fusion marketing partners will help marketers spread the word and reduce their marketing costs.

Step Seven: Launch the Attack

Now it's time to launch the marketing attack. The way to launch it is in slow motion. Don't unleash all of the marketing weapons at once. Launch them one at a time. Guerrillas want to feel comfortable financially that they're not spending too much and emotionally that they don't have too many balls in the air when they launch that attack. My average clients take 18 months to launch a full-scale guerrilla marketing attack. The launching doesn't take place until after those first six steps have been accomplished.

Step Eight: Maintain the Attack

Here's where it gets hard. More money is lost in maintaining the attack than during any other step. It's easy to do the first six steps, but to maintain the attack is difficult, because people expect instant results and marketing does not in most cases deliver instant results. That's why marketers must be patient and maintain their attack.

Marketing plans should be for 10 years, and every six months marketers should reevaluate them to see if they have to make any changes.

If marketers make a marketing plan that's good for one year, they're probably going to make changes to it next year. The correct way for guerrillas to plan is backward. They start with their goal, and then they put in the steps to help them achieve that goal. Therefore, guerrilla marketing means keeping it simple and keeping it brief, because other people in their company are going to read the marketing plan and guerrilla marketers want to get those people on their wavelength. Those people will be able to do that if they read a simple, clear marketing plan.

As good as that plan may be, marketers must think, "This is something that's going to guide me for the next three or five or 10 years." If marketers think in those terms, it's easier to commit to it. Yet, it's necessary to reevaluate a marketing plan every six months to see if there's any tweaking that has to be done. Ideally, guerrillas will be able to make little tweaks and little changes with no major alterations. I tell my clients when they write a marketing plan, "You have to promise to live by this plan for the next three years." Although they swallow hard when I tell them that, they find at the end of the year, after they've made a couple of minor changes, it's easier to go with a plan that's created for three years or five years or longer. Ten years is what marketers should have in mind, because if they have a marketing plan that they think will guide their efforts for the next 10 years, it will be much easier to commit to that plan. Especially in light of the length of time it takes for marketing plans to produce significant results.

I tell my clients that if they do everything right they probably won't see any results from their marketing for the first three months and then they'll see definite results at the end of six months and every month thereafter their profits should continue climbing. A company can't penetrate a person's mind nine times in a short period of time. As a result, guerrilla marketers know it's going to take time. They're not quick to abandon their marketing because it didn't do something the first 30 days or the first 60 days; it hardly ever does.

When most people see a product or a commercial or a marketing message or an email for something they like they're not going to buy it that day. They're going to think about it, they're going to talk to other people about it, they're going to want to see if that company is here to stay. So most people are in the wait-and-see category versus the buy-right-now category. Because of the vast amount of people in the wait-and-see category, marketing takes a while to take hold. If it happens in three months you're pretty darn lucky, and if it doesn't happen after six months then you're probably doing something wrong. But it does take time and it rarely happens instantly unless there is a very special time-dated offer (e.g. You must take advantage of this within the next 15 days or this price will be withdrawn). Marketers may get action from an offer like that, but they can only do that once in a while.

Step Nine: Keep Track

The ninth step is to keep careful track, because guerrillas are going to use a large number of marketing weapons. Some weapons are going to hit the center of the bull's eye, some are going to miss the target entirely. Finding out from each customer what caused them to buy will show which marketing weapons are working and which aren't. So keeping track is crucial.

Step Ten: Make Improvements

Finally, start to improve in all areas. Improve the message, improve the media, improve the budget—which may mean lowering it—and improve the results achieved from the marketing.

Guerrillas who go through those 10 steps will probably succeed on the marketing front. And guerrillas should start marketing as soon as they have a marketing plan, a follow-up plan, and a referral plan, and as soon as all of their employees are able to read those plans and get on that wavelength. And even more important is that once guerrillas start marketing, they realize that a marketing attack is not something that they do once in a while. It's a never-ending process. A process, not an event, and it constantly goes on. Once a company begins marketing it really should never stop. Too many people view marketing as an event, as something that we do now and then or we do when we feel like it or when the economy is right. The reality is, it should always be going on all the time.

Tweaking Your Marketing

Usually, the best and most successful marketing is not created with the first ad or the first direct mail piece. Instead, it's the product of improvements made with minor but crucial changes in details, called tweaking. Tweaking is a significant part of steps eight and ten of launching and implementing a marketing attack.

Embracing the concept of tweaking will dramatically improve the results guerrillas gain from any marketing program, but especially a direct marketing campaign. Great campaigns don't usually get fired from a cannon to hit the center of the target. Instead, they come close to the target and it's tweaking that moves them to the bull's eye.

Tweaking adds firepower to messages.

Tweaking means devoting energy to finding an even better mailing list, an even more cogent message for an envelope or mail subject line, a still better way to state a message. The more research marketers continue to do, the more they'll learn what customers love about their companies— and about their competition.

The best tweakers are the experimenters. Although they may have a winning direct response campaign off and running, they are constantly testing other markets, other messages, other direct marketing methods, tweaking here and there to build their marketing muscle.

Even though repetition is vital for a marketing message to take hold, tweaking can help improve the impact of the message. Take direct marketing as an example. Great results rarely happen instantly in marketing, and that includes direct marketing campaigns. Even the best have to be tweaked or they atrophy with time. The sense of urgency that is so necessary for direct marketers becomes less immediate with repetition. Where repetition is crucial for mass marketing to take hold, it is of lesser importance in direct marketing. Certainly, offers may be repeated, but the line marketers don't want to cross is a lot closer than they think in this arena.

Most guerrillas play an endless game of increasing not only their response rates, but more important, their profits, with each marketing effort they make. Their primary ally is not their budget but their desire to tweak, to improve, to break records. They are not defeated by failures in their experimentation, merely enlightened.

Guerrillas know that records are established to break, not to serve as a permanent standard. That means change is part of the game in order to steadily increase profits. It means new records are being established on a regular basis, not because of major new marketing campaigns, but because of minor improvements on a consistent basis.

Customers are changing and guerrillas are keeping abreast of their new wants and needs, their expectations and hopes. What worked like a miracle last year may be a total loser this year. That direct mail campaign that generated so much profit for one firm last year is being surpassed considerably by its Web site this year. But these marvelous things aren't going to happen because of a flash of genius. Instead, they'll happen because of tweaking and experimentation.

One of the rewards of tweaking is that marketing gets noticed, especially in a society besieged with direct response marketing. Guerrillas are fully aware of the proliferation of direct response marketing in the world today. They see it on their computer monitors, in their mailboxes, on their telephones, on radio, on television, on signs, and in the magazines and newspapers they read. Their awareness gives them the insight that it is more difficult than ever for their snowflake to be noticed in the blizzard. There are countless snowflakes out there, each one enticing and insisting on attention, money, time, and a meeting of the minds. How can guerrillas make their snowflake the one that starts the avalanche of thought that leads to a sale?

Guerrillas begin to answer this from the inside of their prospects' minds. What do they read or watch? What are their foremost interests? It's certain that they do not respond to direct response offers, but that they do respond to what captivates their interest. So marketers must create an offer that is so fascinating to prospects that they are truly enticed. That offer should be more about them than about the product or service. If it looks like all the other direct response pleas, it will be tossed or ignored just as they are. It must stand apart from the other offers being made to them on a non-stop basis. It must be unique to their eye.

Guerrillas accomplish this by using alternate modes of delivery, unique graphics and colors, precision timing, brutal honesty, emotionally-charged verbiage, and a tangible feeling of one-to-one communicating. They never waste the time of their prospects and never try to say everything to everybody, but concentrate instead on saying something to somebody.

Their tweaking includes studying what their competition is doing and then doing it better. They research what marketing tactics are working for others and then adapt these tactics to their own need. They experiment with technology. They learn from customers exactly what motivated them to become customers. Research and patience, along with serious tweaking, help their snowflakes weather the storm.

$ExecRecs$™

EXECUTIVE RECOMMENDATIONS FOR THE BEST PRODUCTS, SERVICES & INTELLIGENCE EXECUTIVES USE TO EXCEL

Featuring the Executive Recommendations of C-Level Leaders (CEO, CFO, CMO, CTO, Partner) From the World's Largest Companies & Firms on Topics Such As:

Favorite Business Books
Favorite Trade Magazine
Favorite Newspaper
Favorite PDA
Favorite Cell Phone
Best Business Travel Airline
Favorite Power Suit
Most Important Technology for the Upcoming Year
Best Business Advice for the Upcoming Year
Best Career Advice for the Upcoming Year
Top 3 Questions to Spur Innovation
And Much, Much More....

Only $14.95 Per Book/Year

To Order, Visit Us At www.Aspatore.com, Fill Out the Order Form Or Call Toll Free 1-866-Aspatore

EXECRECS-ORDER FORM

Call Us Toll Free at 1-866-Aspatore (277-2867)
Or Tear Out This Page and Mail or Fax To:
Aspatore Books, PO Box 883, Bedford, MA 01730
Or Fax To (617) 249-1970 (Preferred)

Name:

E-mail:

Shipping Address:

City: State: Zip:

Billing Address:

City: State: Zip:

Phone:

2 Options-Subscribe or Buy Individual Copies

A) Subscribe-Receive ExecRecs Every Year-And Get Free Shipping & Handling on All Subscriptions!!!!

1 Yr ($14.95)   -   2 Yrs (Save 10%-$26.91) - 5 Yrs (Save 20%-$59.80)
10 Yrs (Save 30%-$104.65) -   Lifetime Subscription ($373.75)

Please List Subscription Length: _____

Would you like us to automatically bill your credit card at the end of your subscription so there is no discontinuity in service? (You can still cancel your subscription at any point before the renewal date.) Please circle: Yes   No

B) Individual Copies

1-2 – No Discount	3-5 – 10% Discount	6-10 – 20% Discount
11-49 – 25% Discount	50-99 – 30% Discount	100-499 – 35% Discount
500+ - 40% Discount		

For orders of 250 or more, customization can be done to the front cover and you can add information or your own ExecRecs to the beginning of the book. Please email store@aspatore.com for more info or call 1-866-Aspatore.

Please List Quantity: _____

(If mailing in a check you can skip this section but please read fine print below and sign below)

Credit Card Type (Visa & Mastercard & Amex):

Credit Card Number:

Expiration Date:

Signature:

*(Please note the billing address much match the address on file with your credit card company exactly) Terms & Conditions-All ExecRecs retail for $14.95. A shipping and handling charge of $3.95 per book will be added, in addition to $.95 for each additional book. If ordering from outside of the US, an additional $8.95 for the first book and $2.95 for each book thereafter will be charged for shipping and handling. Sorry, no returns or refunds or cancellations. Books that are not already published will be shipped upon publication date. Sorry, no returns or refunds at any point unless automatic billing is selected, at which point you may cancel at any time before your subscription is renewed (no funds shall be returned however for the period currently subscribed to). Publication dates are subject to delay.

To Order, Visit Us At www.Aspatore.com, Fill Out the Order Form Or Call Toll Free 1-866-Aspatore

Business Travel Bible & The Business Translator-Ordering Information

Tear Out This Page and Mail or Fax To: Aspatore Books, PO Box 883, Bedford, MA 01730 Or Fax To (617) 249-1970 (Preferred)

Name:

E-mail: Phone:

Shipping Address:

City: State: Zip:

Billing Address:

City: State: Zip:

Individual Copies

1-2 – No Discount   3-5 – 10% Discount   6-10 – 20% Discount   11-49 – 25% Discount   50-99 – 30% Discount   100-499 – 35% Discount   500+ - 40% Discount

For orders of 250 or more, customization can be done to the front cover and you can add information or your own to the beginning of the book. Please email store@aspatore.com for more info or call 1-866-Aspatore.

Business Travel Bible-Please List Quantity: _____
The Business Translator- Please List Quantity: _____

(If mailing in a check you can skip this section but please read fine print below and sign below)

Credit Card Type (Visa & Mastercard & Amex):

Credit Card Number: Expiration Date:

Signature:

*(Please note the billing address much match the address on file with your credit card company exactly)

Terms & Conditions-A shipping and handling charge of $3.95 per book will be added, in addition to $.95 for each additional book. If ordering from outside of the US, an additional $8.95 for the first book and $2.95 for each book thereafter will be charged for shipping and handling. Sorry, no returns or refunds or cancellations. Books that are not already published will be shipped upon publication date.

To Order, Visit Us At www.Aspatore.com, Fill Out the Order Form Or Call Toll Free 1-866-Aspatore

$Career Journal^{TM}$

The CareerJournal™ was developed by leading business executives as the most efficient way to remember key situations, learn from them, and plan for the future. Too many times during the busy course of weeks, months, and years, key events are forgotten, follow-up with contacts and mentors is neglected, and goals are not set. The CareerJournal™ is a way to centralize your thoughts, maintain your contacts, and set goals for your future -- regardless of the current stage of your career. In addition, the CareerJournal™ serves as a timeless reference you can use to collect your ideas and memories throughout the course of your career. Don't let another key event, observation, or job pass you by with out recording it in your CareerJournal™. You never know when it may be useful. Evaluate, plan, and excel with your CareerJournal™.

Only $29.95

What Ifs™

What Ifs is a journal designed to enable business professionals to prepare for the unexpected. The journal features question blocks on topics such as human resources, financials, customers, competitors, partners, and technology, with lined spaces for you to put your answers. Sample questions include: "What if I lose my biggest customer/client?" "What if my most important employee quits?" "What if my competitor cuts their prices in half?" "What if we can no longer offer our biggest selling product/service?" Executives and managers at every level should have one of these filled out and ready to go just in case a "What If" scenario occurs.

Only $14.95

IDEAJOURNAL™

The IdeaJournal™ was developed by leading business executives, politicians, and lawyers as the most efficient way to generate new ideas, develop them, and then execute and bring those ideas to fruition. Too many ideas vanish on pieces of scratch paper or don't even make it onto paper before getting lost among the myriad thoughts in a person's mind. The IdeaJournal™ is an effective way to centralize all your ideas, whether for an entirely new product or service, a way to increase efficiencies, profits, or internal teamwork, or even just a different way to do something. In addition, the IdeaJournal™ can serve as a timeless reference; ideas that you may not be able to use now could be helpful in the future. Don't let another idea pass you by with out recording it in your IdeaJournal™. You never know when it may be useful. Start capitalizing on your ideas with the IdeaJournal™.

Only $29.95

CAREERJOURNAL™ AND IDEAJOURNAL™ AND WHAT IFS™-ORDER FORM

Tear Out This Page and Mail or Fax To: Aspatore Books, PO Box 883, Bedford, MA 01730 Or Fax To (617) 249-1970 (Preferred)

Name:
E-mail: Phone:
Shipping Address:
City: State: Zip:
Billing Address:
City: State: Zip:

Individual Copies-CareerJournal™ ($29.95 Each)

1-2 – No Discount 3-5 – 10% Discount 6-10 – 20% Discount 11-49 – 25% Discount 50-99 – 30% Discount 100-499 – 35% Discount 500+ - 40% Discount

For orders of 250 or more, customization can be done to the front cover and you can add information or your own to the beginning of the journal. Please email store@aspatore.com for more info or call 1-866-Aspatore.

Please List Quantity: _____

Individual Copies-IdeaJournal™ ($29.95 Each)

1-2 – No Discount 3-5 – 10% Discount 6-10 – 20% Discount 11-49 – 25% Discount 50-99 – 30% Discount 100-499 – 35% Discount 500+ - 40% Discount

For orders of 250 or more, customization can be done to the front cover and you can add information or your own to the beginning of the journal. Please email store@aspatore.com for more info or call 1-866-Aspatore.

Please List Quantity: _____

Individual Copies-What Ifs™ ($14.95 Each)

1-2 – No Discount 3-5 – 10% Discount 6-10 – 20% Discount 11-49 – 25% Discount 50-99 – 30% Discount 100-499 – 35% Discount 500+ - 40% Discount

For orders of 250 or more, customization can be done to the front cover and you can add information or your own to the beginning of the journal. Please email store@aspatore.com for more info or call 1-866-Aspatore.

Please List Quantity: _____
(If mailing in a check you can skip this section but please read fine print below and sign below)

Credit Card Type (Visa & Mastercard & Amex):
Credit Card Number: Expiration Date:
Signature:

*(Please note the billing address much match the address on file with your credit card company exactly) Terms & Conditions-A shipping and handling charge of $3.95 per journal will be added, in addition to $.95 for each additional journal. If ordering from outside of the US, an additional $8.95 for the first journal and $2.95 for each journal thereafter will be charged for shipping and handling. Sorry, no returns or refunds or cancellations. Journals that are not already published will be shipped upon publication date.

To Order, Visit Us At www.Aspatore.com, Fill Out the Order Form Or Call Toll Free 1-866-Aspatore

BRAINSTORMERS
INNOVATE, DEVELOP, EXECUTE

Brainstormers™ question blocks and idea-development worksheets are designed by leading business executives as the most efficient way to generate new ideas, develop them, and then execute and bring those ideas to fruition. Too many ideas vanish on pieces of scratch paper or don't even make it to paper before getting lost among the myriad thoughts in a person's mind. Brainstormers™ are an effective way to stimulate your mind to think in new ways and to centralize your ideas, whether for an entirely new product or service, a way to increase efficiencies, profits, or internal teamwork, or even just a way to do something differently.

Available for Individual Purchases or Annual Subscriptions:

Management Brainstormers™

Marketing Brainstormers™

Technology Brainstormers™

Entrepreneurial Brainstormers™

Law Brainstormers™

Only $14.95 Each, Or Subscribe for $59.95 a Year (4 Books)

To Order, Visit Us At www.Aspatore.com, Fill Out the Order Form Or Call Toll Free 1-866-Aspatore

BRAINSTORMERS™-ORDER FORM

Tear Out This Page and Mail or Fax To: Aspatore Books, PO Box 883, Bedford, MA 01730 Or Fax To (617) 249-1970 (Preferred)

Name:
E-mail: Phone:
Shipping Address:
City: State: Zip:
Billing Address:
City: State: Zip:

2 Options-Subscribe or Buy Individual Copies

A) Subscribe-Receive Brainstormers™ Every Quarter - (Please Circle) *Technology - Marketing - Law - Entrepreneur - Management*

1 Yr ($59.95)   -   2 Yrs (Save 20%-$114.88) - 5 Yrs (Save 25%-$269.25)
-   10 Yrs (Save 30%-$502.60) - Lifetime Subscription ($999.95)

Please List Subscription Length: _____

Would you like us to automatically bill your credit card at the end of your subscription so there is no discontinuity in service? (You can still cancel your subscription at any point before the renewal date.) Please circle: Yes   No

B) Individual Copies – (Please Circle) - *Technology - Marketing - Law - Entrepreneur - Management*

1-2 – No Discount ($17.95) 3-5 – 10% Discount 6-10 – 20% Discount 11-49 – 25% Discount 50-99 – 30% Discount 100-499 – 35% Discount 500+ - 40% Discount

For orders of 250 or more, customization can be done to the front cover and you can add information or your own to the beginning of the book. Please email store@aspatore.com for more info or call 1-866-Aspatore. If the type of Brainstormers™ is not circled, it will be assumed you are purchasing the same one as this book.

Please List Quantity: _____
(If mailing in a check you can skip this section but please read fine print below and sign below)

Credit Card Type (Visa & Mastercard & Amex):   Credit
Card Number: Expiration Date:
Signature:

*(Please note the billing address much match the address on file with your credit card company exactly)

Terms & Conditions-A shipping and handling charge of $1.95 per book, per quarter will be added, in addition to$.95 for each additional book ordered. If ordering from outside of the US, an additional $8.95 for the first book, per quarter, and $2.95 for each book thereafter will be charged for shipping and handling. Sorry, no returns or refunds or cancellations. Books that are not already published will be shipped upon publication date. Sorry, no returns or refunds at any point unless automatic billing is selected, at which point you may cancel at any time before your subscription is renewed (no funds shall be returned however for the period currently subscribed to). Publication dates are subject to delay and cancellation at any point.

To Order, Visit Us At www.Aspatore.com, Fill Out the Order Form Or Call Toll Free 1-866-Aspatore

BUILD YOUR OWN BUSINESS LIBRARY

Option A: Receive Every Book Published by Aspatore Books-Only $1,089 a Year- A Savings of Over 60% Off Retail prices

Receive every book published by Aspatore Books every year- between 60-100 books-a must have on bookshelves of every executive and an invaluable resource for quick access, business intelligence from industry insiders. Or send the collection as a gift to someone else!

The Aspatore Business Library Collection features must have business books on various positions, industries and topics, creating the ultimate business library for business professionals. The books in the collection feature business intelligence from C-Level executives (CEO, CTO, CFO, CMO, CFO, Partner) from the world's most respected companies, and represent an invaluable resource for quick access, business intelligence from industry insiders on a wide range of topics. Every business professional should have their own executive library, such as the top executives and great business leaders of our time have always had. The Aspatore Business Library Collection features the most exclusive, biggest name executives of our time and their most insightful words of wisdom, creating the ultimate executive library. Upon order being placed, you will immediately receive books published within the last month, and then for 11 months going forward (you also receive all titles 1-3 months before retail stores receive the new book). You may even request up to 10 books already published by Aspatore Books to be included.

Option B: 25 Best Selling Business Books-Only $399- A Savings of Over 45%Off Retail Prices!

Buy the top 25 best selling business titles published by Aspatore Books, a must have on bookshelves of every executive and an invaluable resource for quick access, business intelligence from industry insiders. Or send the collection as a gift to someone else! These books feature business intelligence from C-Level executives (CEO, CTO, CFO, CMO, CFO, Partner) from over half the world's 500 largest companies. Although every book may not be in your exact area of specialty, having these books on hand will time and again serve as incredible resources for you and everyone in your office. These books provide a wide array of information on various positions, industries and topics, creating a complete business library unto themselves. If you already

To Order, Visit Us At www.Aspatore.com, Fill Out the Order Form Or Call Toll Free 1-866-Aspatore

have one or more of these books, please note this on the order form and different books will be added.

Books Included:

Inside the Minds: The Wireless Industry-Industry Leaders Share Their Knowledge on the Future of the Wireless Revolution

Inside the Minds: Leading Consultants-Industry Leaders Share Their Knowledge on the Future of the Consulting Profession and Industry

Inside the Minds: Leading Deal Makers-Industry Leaders Share Their Knowledge on Negotiations, Leveraging Your Position and the Art of Deal Making

Inside the Minds: The Semiconductor Industry-Industry Leaders Share Their Knowledge on the Future of the Semiconductor Revolution

Inside the Minds: Leading Advertisers-Industry Leaders Share Their Knowledge on the Future of Advertising, Marketing and Building Successful Brands

Inside the Minds: Leading Accountants-Industry Leaders Share Their Knowledge on the Future of the Accounting Industry & Profession

Inside the Minds: The New Health Care Industry-Industry Leaders Share Their Knowledge on the Future of the Technology Charged Health Care Industry

Inside the Minds: Leading IP Lawyers-Leading IP Lawyers Share Their Knowledge on the Art & Science of Intellectual Property

Inside the Minds: Leading Labor Lawyers-Leading Labor Lawyers Share Their Knowledge on the Art & Science of Labor Law

Inside the Minds: Leading Litigators-Leading Litigators Share Their Knowledge on the Art & Science of Litigation

Inside the Minds: The Art of Public Relations-PR Visionaries Reveal the Secrets to Getting Noticed, Making a Name for Your Company, and Building a Brand Through Public Relations

Inside the Minds: Venture Capitalists-Inside the High Stakes and Fast Moving World of Venture Capital

Inside the Minds: Leading Investment Bankers-An Inside Look at the Art & Science of Investment Banking

Bigwig Briefs: Hunting Venture Capital-An Inside Look at the Basics of Venture Capital

Inside the Minds: Leading Wall St. Investors-Financial Gurus Reveal the Secrets to Picking a Winning Portfolio

Inside the Minds: Leading Marketers-Industry Leaders Share Their Knowledge on Building Successful Brands

Inside the Minds: Chief Technology Officers-Industry Experts Reveal the Secrets to Developing, Implementing, and Capitalizing on the Best Technologies in the World

Inside the Minds: Entrepreneurial Momentum-Jump Starting a New Business Venture and Gaining Traction for Businesses of All Sizes to Take the Step to the Next Level

Inside the Minds: The Entrepreneurial Problem Solver-Getting Yourself & Others to Think More Like an Entrepreneur

Inside the Minds: The Telecommunications Industry-The Future of Telecommunications – Opportunities, Risks & Areas to Watch

Inside the Minds: Leading CEOs-The Secrets to Management, Leadership & Profiting in Any Economy

Inside the Minds: Building a $1,000,000 Nest Egg-Financial Gurus Reveal the Secrets for Anyone to Build a $1,000,000 Nest Egg on Their Own Terms

Inside the Minds: Leading CTOs-Industry Leaders Share Their Knowledge on Harnessing and Developing the Best Technologies

Bigwig Briefs: Guerrilla Marketing-The Best of Guerrilla Marketing

Term Sheets & Valuations-An Inside Look at the Intricacies of Term Sheets & Valuations

Business Library Code 042202

To Order, Visit Us At www.Aspatore.com, Fill Out the Order Form Or Call Toll Free 1-866-Aspatore

BUILD YOUR OWN BUSINESS LIBRARY

Tear Out This Page and Mail or Fax To: Aspatore Books, PO Box 883, Bedford, MA 01730 Or Fax To (617) 249-1970 (Preferred)

Name:

E-mail:

Shipping Address:

City: State: Zip:

Billing Address:

City: State: Zip:

Phone:

Please Check Option A or Option B:

Option A _____ (Receive Every Book Published by Aspatore Books-$1,089 a Year)

Please indicate here any titles already published by Aspatore Books you would like in addition (there will be no charge for these titles as they will be included as part of the first month of books):

_____

_____

_____

_____

Option B _____ (25 Best Selling Business Books-$399)

Please indicate here any titles you already currently have (other best selling titles on a similar topic will then be added in their place):

_____

_____

(If mailing in a check you can skip this section but please read fine print below and sign below)

Credit Card Type (Visa & Mastercard & Amex):

Credit Card Number:

Expiration Date:

Signature:

If option A is chosen, would you like us to automatically bill your credit card at the end of your subscription so there is no discontinuity in service? (You can still cancel your subscription at any point before the renewal date.) Please check: Yes _____   No _____

*(Please note the billing address much match the address on file with your credit card company exactly) Terms & Conditions-We shall send a confirmation receipt to your e-mail address. If ordering from Massachusetts, please add 5% sales tax on the order (not including shipping and handling). If ordering from outside of the US, an additional $300 in shipping and handling costs will be charged for Option A and an additional $125 for Option B. All books are paperback and will be shipped as soon as they become available. Total number of books for Option A will vary from year to year, between 60-100 books. Sorry, no returns or refunds at any point unless automatic billing is selected, at which point you may cancel at any time before your subscription is renewed (no funds shall be returned however for the period currently subscribed to). Books that are not already published will be shipped upon publication date. Publication dates are subject to delay-please allow 1-2 weeks for delivery of first books. For the most up to date information on publication dates and availability please visit www.Aspatore.com.

To Order, Visit Us At www.Aspatore.com, Fill Out the Order Form Or Call Toll Free 1-866-Aspatore

THE FOCUSBOOK™

ASSEMBLE YOUR OWN BUSINESS BOOK™

Ever wish you could assemble your own business book, and even add your own thoughts in the book? Here is your chance to become the managing editor or your own book!

The Focusbook™ enables you to become the managing editor of your own book, by selecting individual chapters from the best selling business books published by Aspatore Books to assemble your own business book. A Focusbook™ can highlight a particular topic, industry, or area of expertise for yourself, your team, your course, or even your entire company. You can even add additional text of your own to the book, such as reference information, points to focus on, or even a course syllabus, in order to further customize it to better suit your needs. The Focusbook™ is the future of business books, allowing you to become the managing editor of your own business book, based on what you deem important, enabling yourself, and others to focus, innovate and outperform.

How It Works:

1. Select up to 10, 15, or 25 chapters from the choices on the following pages by checking the appropriate boxes. (Each Chapter Ranges From 15-40 Pages)
2. Decide if you want to include any of your own text to the book-maybe an introduction (as to why you chose these chapters), employee instructions (for new hires or to use as a management course/refresher), a course syllabus, information so it is applicable for clients/customers (reference), or even an article/white paper you already wrote. (Please note Aspatore Books will not edit the work, it is simply printed as is. Aspatore Books will not be considered the publisher of any additions and you will retain all rights to that content.)
3. Decide on a quantity.

To Order, Visit Us At www.Aspatore.com, Fill Out the Order Form Or Call Toll Free 1-866-Aspatore

How the Book Will Look:

1. The book will be 5 inches tall and 8 inches wide (on the front and back). The width will vary depending on the amount of text. The book will look like a normal business book found in bookstores nationwide.

2. On the cover of the book, it will read "A Focusbook™ Assembled By," with your name on the next line (Jason Phillips in the example above). We can also add a company/university/course name if you so choose. Your name will also appear on the spine of the book. You can then also select a title for your Focusbook™ (such as Marketing Smarts as depicted in the picture above). On the back of the book will be the chapter names from your book.

3. The book will feature the standard Focusbook™ cover (see above), with the dominant colors being black with a red stripe across.

4. The chapters will be placed in a random order, unless a specific order is instructed on the order form. If you are adding your own text, it can be placed at the beginning or the end of the text.

5. The book will feature the chapters you selected, plus any content of your own (optional), and a special section at the end for notes and ideas of your own to add as you read through and refer back to your Focusbook™.

Select the Chapters You Want on the Following Pages
Then Fill Out the Order Form at the End

To Order, Visit Us At www.Aspatore.com, Fill Out the Order Form Or Call Toll Free 1-866-Aspatore

Chapter Title	Author	Units

VENTURE CAPITAL/ENTREPRENEURSHIP

MARKETING/ADVERTISING/PR

*Denotes Best Selling Chapter

Chapter Title	Author	Units

MANAGEMENT/ CONSULTING

*Denotes Best Selling Chapter

Chapter Title	Author	Units

LAW

75. *Navigating Labor Law, Charles Birenbaum (Thelan Reid & Priest, Labor Chair), 1
76. The Makings of a Great Labor Lawyer, Gary Klotz (Butzel Long, Labor Chair), 1
77. The Complexity of Labor Law, Michael Reynvaan (Perkins Coie, Labor Chair), 1
78. *Labor Lawyer Code: Integrity and Honesty, Max Brittain, Jr. (Schiff Hardin & Waite, Labor Chair), 1
89. The Litigator: Advocate and Counselor, Rob Johnson (Sonnenschein Nath, Litigation Chair), 1
90. *Keys to Success in Litigation: Empathy, John Strauch (Jones, Day, Reavis & Pogue, Litigation Chair), 1
91. *Major Corporate and Commercial Litigation, Jeffrey Barist (Milbank, Tweed, Hadley, Litigation Chair), 1
92. Keys to Success as a Litigator, Martin Flumenbaum (Paul, Weiss, Rifkind, Litigation Chair), 1
93. *Deciding When to Go to Trial, Martin Lueck (Robins, Kaplan, Miller, Litigation Chair), 1
94. Credibility and Persuasiveness in Litigation, Michael Feldberg (Schulte Roth & Zabel, Litigation Chair), 1
95. *Litigation Challenges, Thomas Kilbane (Squire, Sanders, Dempsey, Litigation Chair), 1
96. *Keeping it Simple, Evan R. Chesler (Cravath, Swaine & Moore, Litigation Chair), 1
97. Assessing Risk Through Preparation & Honesty, Harvey Kurzweil (Dewey Ballantine, Litigation Chair), 1
98. The Essence of Success, James W. Quinn (Weil, Gotshal & Manges, Litigation Chair), 1
99. The Performance Aspect of Litigation, Charles E. Koob (Simpson Thacher Bartlett, Litigation Chair), 1
100. *The Future of IP: Intellectual Asset Mngmnt., Richard S. Florsheim (Foley & Lardner, IP Chair), 1
101. The Balancing of Art & Science in IP Law, Victor M. Wigman (Blank Rome, IP Chair), 1
102. *Policing a Trademark, Paula J. Krasny (Baker & McKenzie, IP Chair), 1
103. Credibility & Candor: Must Have Skills, Brandon Baum (Cooley Godward, IP Litigation Chair), 1
104. The Art & Science of Patent Law, Stuart Lubitz (Hogan & Hartson, Partner), 1
105. Successful IP Litigation, Cecilia Gonzalez (Howrey Simon Arnold & White, IP Chair), 1
106. Achieving Recognized Value in Ideas, Dean Russell (Kilpatrick Stockton, IP Chair), 1
108. Keeping Current W/ Changing Times, Bruce Keller (Debevoise & Plimpton, IP Litigation Chair), 1
109. *Maximizing the Value of an IP Portfolio, Roger Maxwell (Jenkins & Gilchrist, IP Chair), 2
110. * Experience in Deal Making, Joseph Hoffman (Arter & Hadden, Corporate/Securities Chair), 1
111. *The Art of the Deal, Mark Macenka (Testa, Hurwitz & Thibeault, Business Chair), 1
112. Communicating With Clients, Gerard S. DiFiore (Reed Smith, Corporate/Securities Chair), 1
113. Making a Deal Work, Kenneth S. Bezozo (Haynes and Boone, Business Chair), 1
114. Challenges for Internet & Tech. Companies, Carl Cohen (Buchanan Ingersoll, Technology Chair), 1
115. The Copyright Revolution, Mark Fischer (Palmer & Dodge, Internet/E-Commerce Chair), 1
116. Privacy Rights and Ownership of Content, Brian Vandenberg (uBid.com, General Counsel), 1
117. Business Intelligence From Day One, Mark I. Gruhin (Schmeltzer, Aptaker and Shepard, , Partner), 1
118. Legal Rules for Internet Companies, Arnold Levine (Proskauer Rose LLP, Chair, iPractice Group), 1
119. Protecting Your Assets, Gordon Caplan (Mintz Levin PC), 1
120. The Golden Rules of Raising Capital, James Hutchinson (Hogan & Hartson LLP), 1
121. Identifying the Right Legal Challenges, John Igeo (Encore Development, General Counsel), 1
122. The Importance of Patents, Richard Turner (Sughrue, Mion,, Senior Counsel), 1
79. *Common Values in Employment Law, Columbus Gangemi, Jr. (Winston & Strawn, Labor Chair), 1
80. Building Long Term Relationships with Clients, Fred Alvarez (Wilson Sonsini, Labor Chair), 1
81. *Becoming Part of the Client's Success, Brian Gold (Sidley Austin Brown & Wood, Labor Chair), 1
82. *Understanding Multiple Audiences, Raymond Wheeler (Morrison & Foerster, Labor Chair), 1
83. Employment Lawyer: Advisor & Advocate, Judy Langevin (Gray, Plant, Mooty & Bennett, Labor Chair), 1
84. *Bringing Added Value to the Deal, Mary Ann Jorgenson (Squires Sanders Dempsey,Labor Chair), 1
85. Traditional Legal Matters on the Internet, Harrison Smith (Krooth & Altman LLP, Partner), 1

TECHNOLOGY/INTERNET

167. *Closing the Technology Gap, Dr. Carl S. Ledbetter (Novell, CTO), 1
168. *Creating and Enriching Business Value, Richard Schroth (Perot Systems, CTO), 1
169. *Innovation Drives Business Success, Kirill Tatarinov (BMC Software, Senior Vice President), 1
170. *Managing the Technology Knowledge, Dr. Scott Dietzen (BEA E-Commerce Server Division, CTO), 1
171. The CTO as an Agent of Change, Doug Cavit (McAfee.com, CTO), 1
172. The Class Struggle and The CTO, Dan Woods (Capital Thinking, CTO), 1
173. A CTO's Perspective on the Role of a CTO, Mike Toma (eLabor, CTO), 1
174. Technology Solutions to Business Needs, Michael S. Dunn (Encoda Systems, CTO, EVP), 1
175. Bridging Business and Technology, Mike Ragunas (StaplesDirect.com, CTO), 1
176. *The Art of Being a CTO - Fostering Change, Rick Bergquist (PeopleSoft, CTO), 1
178. Developing Best of Breed Technologies, Dr. David Whelan (Boeing, Space and Communications, CTO), 1

*Denotes Best Selling Chapter

Chapter Title	Author	Units
179. *Technology as a Strategic Weapon, Kevin Vasconi (Covisint, CTO),		1
180. Role of the CTO in a Venture-Backed Startup, Dan Burgin (Finali, CTO),		1
181. Leading Technology During Turbulent Times, Frank Campagnoni (GE Global eXchange Services, CTO),		1
276. Success Begins & Ends With Customers, Richard Notebart (Tellabs, CEO),		1
277. *Success is Persistence, Passion & Perspiration, David Struwas (DSL.net, CEO),		1
279. *Successful Telecom, Here and Overseas, K. Paul Singh (Primus Telecommunications Group, CEO),		1
280. Managing in Telecommunications, Alex Mashinsky (QOptics and Arbinet-theexchange, Founder),		1
281. Staying on Course: Telco Navigation, John Schofield (Advanced Fibre Communications, CEO),		1
282. Surviving to Success, Danny Stroud (AppliedTheory, CEO),		1
283. High-Speed Management, David Trachtenberg (StarBand Communications, CEO),		1
284. Leadership in Telecommunications, Gordon Blankstein (Global Light Telecommunications, CEO),		1
285. Winning on the Basics: Right People, Values, Jeff Allen (IntelliSpace, CEO),		1
286. Watching Information Flow, Art Zeile (Inflow, CEO),		1
147. *Wireless Technology: Make It Simple , John Zeglis (AT&T Wireless, CEO),		1
148. *Bringing Value to the Consumer, Patrick McVeigh (OmniSky, Chairman and CEO),		1
149. Wireless Challenges, Sanjoy Malik (Air2Web, Founder, President and CEO),		1
150. The High Costs of Wireless, Paul Sethy (AirPrime, Founder & Chairman),		1
151. Developing Areas of Wireless, Reza Ahy (Aperto Networks, President & CEO),		1
152. *The Real Potential for Wireless, Martin Cooper (Arraycomm, Chairman & CEO),		1
153. Bringing Wireless into the Mainstream, Robert Gemmell (Digital Wireless, CEO),		1
154. VoiceXML, Alex Laats (Informio, CEO and Co-Founder),		1
155. Reaching the Epitome of Productivity, Rod Hoo (LGC Wireless, President and CEO),		1
157. The Wireless Satellite Space , Tom Moore (WildBlue, President and CEO)		1
158. *Memory Solutions for Semiconductor Industry, Steven R. Appleton (Micron Technology, Inc., CEO),		1
159. *Programmable Logic: The Digital Revolution, Wim Roelandts (Xilinx, Inc., CEO),		1
160. The Streaming Media Future, Jack Guedj, Ph.D. (Tvia, Inc., President),		1
161. Building a Winning Semiconductor Company, Igor Khandros, Ph.D. (FormFactor, President and CEO),		1
162. The Next Generation Silicon Lifestyle, Rajeev Madhavan (Magma, Chairman, CEO and President),		1
163. Semiconductors: The Promise of the Future, Steve Hanson (ON Semiconductor, President and CEO),		1
164. Dynamics of the Semiconductor Data Center , Eyal Waldman (Mellanox Technologies, LTD, CEO),		1
165. The Market-Driven Semiconductor Industry, Bob Lynch (Nitronex, President and CEO),		1
166. Semiconductors: Meeting Performance Demand, Satish Gupta (Cradle Technologies, President and CEO),		1

FINANCIAL

244. *Merging Information Tech. & Accounting, Paul McDonald (Robert Half Int'l, Executive Director),		1
245. *The Accountant's Perspective, Gerald Burns (Moss Adams, Partner),		2
247. *Audits & Analyzing Business Processes, Lawrence Rieger (Andersen, Global Managing Partner),		1
250. E-Business Transformation, Fred Round (Ernst & Young, Director of eBusiness Tax),		1
251. Accounting: The UK/US Perspective, Colin Cook (KPMG, Head of Transaction Services - London),		1
252. The Changing Role of the Accountant, Jim McKerlie (Ran One, CEO),		1
253. The Future of Accounting, Harry Steinmetz (M.R. Weiser & Company, Partner),		1

INVESTING

197. Who Wants to Become a Millionaire?, Laura Lee Wagner (American Express, Senior Advisor),		1
198. *The Gold is in Your Goals, Harry R. Tyler (Tyler Wealth Counselors, Inc., CEO),		1
199. *Timeless Tips for Building Your Nest Egg, Christopher P. Parr (Financial Advantage, Inc.),		1
200. It's What You Keep, Not Make, That Counts, Jerry Wade (Wade Financial Group, President),		1
201. Accumulating Your Million-Dollar Nest Egg, Marc Singer (Singer Xenos Wealth Management),		1
228. Time-Honored Investment Principles, Marilyn Bergen (CMC Advisors, LLC, Co-President),		1
229. *The Art & Science of Investing, Clark Blackman, II (Post Oak Capital Advisors, Managing Dir.),		1
240. Altering Investment Strategy for Retirement, Gary Mandell (The Mandell Group, President),		1
241. *Fair Value & Unfair Odds in Investing, Scott Opsal (Invista Capital Mngmt, Chief Investment Officer),		1
242. Earnings Count & Risk Hurts, Victoria Collins (Keller Group Investment Mngmnt, Principal),		1
243. *Navigating Turbulent Markets, Howard Weiss (Bank of America, Senior Vice President),		1
249. Building an All-Weather Portfolio, Sanford Axelroth & Robert Studin (First Financial Group),		1
254. Managing Your Wealth in Any Market, Gilda Borenstein (Merill Lynch, Wealth Mngmt. Advisor),		1
255. Winning Strategies for International Investing, Josephine Jiménez (Montgomery Asset, Principal),		1
256. The Psychology of a Successful Investor, Robert G. Morris(Lord Abbett, Dir. of Equity Investments),		1
257. *Investing for a Sustainable Future, Robert Allan Rikoon (Rikoon-Carret Investments, CEO),		1

*Denotes Best Selling Chapter

THE FOCUSBOOK™
ASSEMBLE YOUR OWN BUSINESS BOOK™

Call Us Toll Free at 1-866-Aspatore (277-2867)
Or Tear Out the Next 2 Order Form Pages & Fax or Mail BOTH Pages To:
Aspatore Books, PO Box 883, Bedford, MA 01730
Or Fax To (617) 249-1970 (Preferred)

Name:
Email:
Shipping Address:
City: State: Zip:
Billing Address:
City: State: Zip:
Phone:
Book Content-5 Questions
1. What chapters would you like added? (Please list by number and author last name-i.e. 2-Jones.) (10 Units/Chapters is Standard for 1 Book.):

_____
_____
_____
_____
_____

2. If you are adding content, do you want it put at the beginning or end of the book? _____

3. Would you like the chapters in a particular order? (If this part is not filled out, we shall put them in random order.) If so, please list by author in order from first to last:

_____
_____
_____
_____

4. How would you like your name to read on the cover? (If you would like a company/university/course name added as well, please list it here with your name.): _____

5. What would you like the title of the book to be? (If none is added, we will simply put the information from the previous question.):

_____

To Order, Visit Us At www.Aspatore.com, Fill Out the Order Form Or Call Toll Free 1-866-Aspatore

Pricing-3 Steps

1. Quantity:

1 Book – $99   **2 Books** – $198 ($99 Per Book)
5 Books – $445 ($89 Per Book)   **10 Books** – $790 ($79 Per Book)
50 Books – $2,450 ($49 Per Book) **100 Books** – $3,900 ($39 Per Book)
250 Books – $7,250 ($29 Per Book)   **500 Books** – $10,500 ($21 Per Book)
1000 Books – $15,000 ($15 Per Book) **5000 Books** – $49,750 ($9.95 Per Book)

Number of Books: _____   Price for Books: _____

2. Decide the Number of Chapters in Your Book (If you are selecting only 10 units or less, please skip to No. 3-units are based on number of pages-most chapters are 1 unit, however some are more depending on length.)

10 Units (Standard-Approximately 200-250 Pages) – No Extra Charge
15 Units – Please Add $25 Per Book if Ordering Between 1-10 Books, Add $15 Per Book if Ordering 50-250 Books, Add $7.50 Per Book if Ordering 500-5000 Books (So if ordering 50 books, the additional charge would be 50x10=$500)
25 Units – Please Add $75 Per Book if Ordering Between 1-10 Books, Add $25 Per Book if Ordering 50-250 Books, Add $10 Per Book if Ordering 500-5000 Books (So if ordering 50 books, the additional charge would be 50x25=$1,250)

Number of Units: _____   Price for Additional Chapters: _____

3. Adding Content (You must order at least 50 books to add content.) (If you are not adding any content, skip this section.)

Adding 1 Page – Please Add $3 Per Book if Ordering 50-250 Books, Please Add $2 Per Book if Ordering 500-5000 Books
Adding 2-9 Pages – *Please Add $8 Per Book if Ordering 50-250* Books, Add $4.00 Per Book if Ordering 500-5000 Books
Adding 10-49 Pages – Please Add $18 Per Book if Ordering 50-250 Books, Add $9 Per Book if Ordering 500-5000 Books
Adding 50-99 Pages – Please Add $25 Per Book if Ordering 50-250 Books, Add $13 Per Book if Ordering 500-5000 Books
Adding 100-149 Pages – Please Add $40 Per Book if Ordering 50-250 Books, Add $20 Per Book if Ordering 500-5000 Books

(Please base page count by single spacing, 12 point font, Times New Roman font type on 8.5X11 paper.) (Only charts and graphs that are smaller than 4 inches wide and 7 inches tall can be included.)
(A staff member will email you within 1 week of the order being placed to coordinate receiving the materials electronically.)

Number of Pages Added: _____   Price for Pages Added: _____

To Order, Visit Us At www.Aspatore.com, Fill Out the Order Form Or Call Toll Free 1-866-Aspatore

PLEASE REPRINT THE FOLLOWING INFORMATION FROM THE PREVIOUS PAGE:

Number of Books: _____   **Price for Books:** _____
Number of Units: _____   **Price for Additional Chapters:** _____
Number of Pages Added: _____   **Price for Pages Added:** _____

Total Price From Sections 1-3: _____

(If mailing in a check you can skip this section but please read fine print below and sign below-check must be received before a book is started-please email jennifer@aspatore.com for an alternate address if you are going to send the check via FedEx or UPS as the PO Box will not accept such shipments.)

Credit Card Type (Visa & Mastercard & Amex):

Credit Card Number:

Expiration Date:

Signature (Acceptance of Order and Terms & Conditions): _____

IF ADDING CONTENT, AFTER FAXING/MAILING THIS FORM, PLEASE EMAIL THE CONTENT AS A MICROSOFT WORD ATTACHMENT TO JENNIFER@ASPATORE.COM. THE EMAIL SHOULD INCLUDE YOUR NAME AND FOCUS BOOK NAME. YOU WILL RECEIVE AN EMAIL BACK WITHIN 24 HOURS IF THERE ARE ANY PROBLEMS/QUESTIONS FROM OUR STAFF.

*(Please note the billing address much match the address on file with your credit card company exactly)

For rush orders, guaranteed to ship within 1 week (for orders of 10 books or less) or within 2 weeks (for orders of 50 books or more) please initial here _____. An additional charge of $100 for orders of 10 or less books, $250 for orders of 11-25 books, $500 for orders of 25-100 books will be charged. If additional information is needed on rush orders, please email jennifer@aspatore.com.

If you would like your order sent via FedEx or UPS, for faster delivery, please enter your FedEx or UPS number here: _____ Please Circle One (FedEx/UPS).
Delivery Type-Please Circle (Next Day, 2Day/Ground)

Terms & Conditions - Prices include shipping and handling, unless a rush order is placed. All books are sent via media mail. We shall send a confirmation receipt to your email address. If ordering from Massachusetts, please add 5% sales tax on the order. If ordering from outside of the US, an additional $8.95 for shipping and handling costs will be charged for the first book, and $1.95 for each book thereafter. All books are paperback and will be shipped as soon as they become available. Sorry, no returns, refunds or cancellations at any point, even before the order has shipped or any additional content submitted. Aspatore Books is also not liable for any spacing errors in the book-only printing errors as determined by Aspatore Books. Any additions to the book will be formatted in relation to the rest of the text font size and type. Publication dates are subject to delay-please allow 1-4 weeks for delivery.

Please note that the rights to any content added to the Focusbook™ shall be retained by the author, and that Aspatore Books is simply printing the material in the Focusbook™, not publishing it. Aspatore Books shall not print, publish or distribute the content in any other media, or sell or distribute the content. The rights to all other material in the book shall remain the property of Aspatore Books and may not be reproduced or resold under any condition with out the express written consent of Aspatore Books. The author warrants and represents that to the best of his/her knowledge: (a) he/she has the right to print this material; (b) he/she has no contractual commitment of any kind which may prevent him/her from printing the material; (c) the contribution does not contain any unlawful, libelous or defamatory matter and does not infringe upon the rights, including copyright, of any other person or entity. The individual adding content to the Focusbook™ agrees to assume full liability for any content added to their FocusBook™, and agrees to indemnify and hold harmless Aspatore Books, its owners, officers, employees, agents, shareholders, parents, affiliates, subsidiaries, predecessors, agents, legal representatives, successors and assignees for and against any and all suits, claims, damages, liabilities, including attorneys' fees, based on or with respect to the falsity of any representation or warranty made to Aspatore Books, whether actual or claimed, or any infringement or related claims.

To Order, Visit Us At www.Aspatore.com, Fill Out the Order Form Or Call Toll Free 1-866-Aspatore

Bigwig Briefs: Become a CTO-Leading CTOs Reveal How to Get There, Stay There, and Empower Others That Work With You (ISBN: 1587620715)
Bigwig Briefs: Small Business Internet Advisor-Big Business Secrets for Small Business Success on the Internet (ISBN: 1587620189)
Inside the Minds: Internet Marketing-Advertising, Marketing and Building a Successful Brand on the Internet (ISBN: 1587620022)
Inside the Minds: Internet Bigwigs-Leading Internet CEOs and Research Analysts Forecast the Future of the Internet Economy (ISBN: 1587620103)
Inside the Minds: Internet CFOs-Information Every Individual Should Know About the Financial Side of Internet Companies (ISBN: 158762)
Inside the Minds: Internet BizDev-The Golden Rules to Inking Deals in the Internet Industry (ISBN: 1587620057)
Bigwig Briefs: The Golden Rules of the Internet Economy-The Future of the Internet Economy (Even After the Shakedown) (ISBN: 1587620138)
Inside the Minds: Internet Lawyers-Important Answers to Issues For Every Entrepreneur, Lawyer & Anyone With a Web Site (ISBN: 1587620065)

LAW

Inside the Minds: Leading Labor Lawyers-Labor Chairs Reveal the Secrets to the Art & Science of Labor Law (ISBN: 1587621614)
Inside the Minds: Leading Litigators-Litigation Chairs Revel the Secrets to the Art & Science of Litigation (ISBN: 1587621592)
Inside the Minds: Leading IP Lawyers-IP Chairs Reveal the Secrets to the Art & Science of IP Law (ISBN: 1587621606)
Inside the Minds: Leading Deal Makers-Negotiations, Leveraging Your Position and the Art of Deal Making (ISBN: 1587620588)
Inside the Minds: Internet Lawyers-Important Answers to Issues For Every Entrepreneur, Lawyer & Anyone With a Web Site (ISBN: 1587620065)
Bigwig Briefs: The Art of Deal Making-The Secrets to the Deal Making Process (ISBN: 1587621002)
Bigwig Briefs: Career Options for Law School Students-Leading Partners Reveal the Secrets to Choosing the Best Career Path (ISBN: 1587621010)

MARKETING/ADVERTISING/PR

Inside the Minds: Leading Marketers-Leading Chief Marketing Officers Reveal the Secrets to Building a Billion Dollar Brand (ISBN: 1587620537)
Inside the Minds: Leading Advertisers-Advertising CEOs Reveal the Tricks of the Advertising Profession (ISBN: 1587620545)
Inside the Minds: The Art of PR-Leading PR CEOs Reveal the Secrets to the Public Relations Profession (ISBN: 1587620634)
Inside the Minds: PR Visionaries-The Golden Rules of PR and Becoming a Senior Level Advisor With Your Clients (ISBN: 1587621517)

To Order, Visit Us At www.Aspatore.com, Fill Out the Order Form Or Call Toll Free 1-866-Aspatore

Inside the Minds: Internet Marketing-Advertising, Marketing and Building a Successful Brand on the Internet (ISBN: 1587620022)
Bigwig Briefs: Online Advertising-Successful and Profitable Online Advertising Programs (ISBN: 1587620162)
Bigwig Briefs: Guerrilla Marketing -The Best of Guerrilla Marketing-Big Marketing Ideas For a Small Budget (ISBN: 1587620677)
Bigwig Briefs: Become a VP of Marketing-How to Get There, Stay There, and Empower Others That Work With You (ISBN: 1587620707)

FINANCIAL

Inside the Minds: Leading Accountants-The Golden Rules of Accounting & the Future of the Accounting Industry and Profession (ISBN: 1587620529)
Inside the Minds: Internet CFOs-Information Every Individual Should Know About the Financial Side of Internet Companies (ISBN: 1587620057)
Inside the Minds: The Financial Services Industry-The Future of the Financial Services Industry & Professions (ISBN: 1587620626)
Inside the Minds: Leading Investment Bankers-Leading I-Bankers Reveal the Secrets to the Art & Science of Investment Banking (ISBN: 1587620618)
Bigwig Briefs: Become a CFO-Leading CFOs Reveal How to Get There, Stay There, and Empower Others That Work With You (ISBN: 1587620731)
Bigwig Briefs: Become a VP of Biz Dev-How to Get There, Stay There, and Empower Others That Work With You (ISBN: 1587620723)
Bigwig Briefs: Career Options for MBAs-I-Bankers, Consultants & CEOs Reveal the Secrets to Choosing the Best Career Path (ISBN: 1587621029)

INVESTING

Inside the Minds: Building a $1,000,000 Nest Egg -Simple, Proven Ways for Anyone to Build a $1M Nest Egg On Your Own Terms (ISBN: 1587622157)
Inside the Minds: Leading Wall St. Investors -The Best Investors of Wall Street Reveal the Secrets to Profiting in Any Economy (ISBN: 1587621142)

OTHER

Inside the Minds: The New Health Care Industry-The Future of the Technology Charged Health Care Industry (ISBN: 1587620219)
Inside the Minds: The Real Estate Industry-The Future of Real Estate and Where the Opportunities Will Lie (ISBN: 1587620642)
Inside the Minds: The Telecommunications Industry-Telecommunications Today, Tomorrow and in 2030 (ISBN: 1587620669)
Inside the Minds: The Automotive Industry-Leading CEOs Share Their Knowledge on the Future of the Automotive Industry (ISBN: 1587620650)

To Order, Visit Us At www.Aspatore.com, Fill Out the Order Form Or Call Toll Free 1-866-Aspatore

ASPATORE

Executive Business Intelligence